ADVANCE PRAISE

I could have never imagined John's impact on my business and personal life. He has this uncanny ability to say precisely what you need to hear at the right moment. I can't imagine doing life without having him by my side for counsel. John has always selflessly given his time to help people. He is a great man and friend. Only his heavenly reward can repay him for the countless lives he has touched.

                                                        –Robbie McDaniel, CEO

There isn't a week that goes by that I don't find myself repeating the words and wisdom of John Richie.

                                                        –Benj Miller, CEO

Time spent with John has produced an abundance of fruit, not only for me but also for those in my sphere of influence. John is a deep thinker and has coached me to think deeply. He has helped me challenge the demands of life and not settle for the shallow end of the pool. John's coaching has fostered growth in my walk with Christ, relationships, financial literacy, businesses, and network. John Richie enriches my life.

                                                        –Eric James, CEO

I've been CEO of Insight Global for six-and-a-half years, and John has been my coach the entire time. His wisdom is invaluable. He challenged me on our company's lack of clear values and purpose. He coached me on discovering values with my team and scaling them across the company. Our "Shared Values" have had a multi-billion-dollar impact on my company. He challenges me and holds me accountable as a Christian leader. During our time together, John has walked me through tough decisions and has always been someone to whom I can turn. Quite simply, I wouldn't be the CEO I am today, and Insight Global wouldn't be the company it is without John's influence on me.

                                                        –Bert Bean, CEO

A conversation with John Richie is something to look forward to, prepare for, and cherish. John has been my business coach for over fifteen years. During that time, he has helped me navigate acquisitions, opportunities, personnel challenges, growth, and a successful exit. Not to mention, he has supported me through countless personal challenges in my own life.

For me, John has been more than a coach; he's been a mentor, minister, advisor, historian, psychologist, and therapist. This book bottles up the wisdom, insights, challenges, and affirmations many of us have benefited from in our relationships with John. Therefore, it is nothing less than a gift.

John's influence on my life has been profound. The fact that I can recommend this book to a thousand people at once makes John's impact scalable in an extraordinary way. I am so thankful that he has written this.

-Eric Dykes, EVP

John Richie is truly a godly man of wisdom. He is my mentor, coach, and friend. I cannot express my utmost gratitude for the proverbial discernment he has given me, not only in my business but also in how it intersects with my marriage, family, and ministry. Rarely can you find someone who meets you where you are, both in good and struggling times, providing critical insights into where your heart rests and how that affects your decisions and actions.

John focuses on reaching the core of your faith with God first and how that manifests into the key priorities in your life. I have experienced first-hand how his ability to help me refocus my attention on God has altered all facets of my life so that it glorifies God and benefits those around me. Thank you, John, for your care and wisdom.

-Brian Yee, CEO

John Richie is a highly esteemed leader and mentor whose profound influence has significantly shaped my personal and professional development. His wisdom, deeply anchored in Scripture, extensive academic studies, and rich tapestry of life experiences, has guided me and numerous other men and their families. Beyond his expertise as a business coach, John excels as a trusted life coach, enriching lives through his prolific writings and impactful teachings. His contributions to the field are substantial, and his insights are invaluable. When John speaks or writes, it is imperative to pay attention, as his wisdom invariably offers significant benefits.

-Greg Bishop, CEO

I met John in January of 2019. He mentored me and five other men on a twelve-month Radical Mentoring journey. Five years later, while John remains a mentor, he has also become a friend. His wisdom and insight have guided decisions that have impacted my marriage, family, friendships, and co-workers. While John's wisdom is undeniable, his peace and unwavering faith have brought validity and comfort to his words. John lovingly challenged me, and I am thankful for his friendship. John signs off at the end of each email with "Truth and Grace"—a simple but powerful summation of what I've experienced and learned from him.

-Justin Walker, CFO

I've known John for over twelve years. The depth of his impact on and through my life cannot be measured. John has been my guide through numerous significant life events: marriage, kids, failed adoption, deaths, business success and turmoil, and more. He has consistently demonstrated love, grace, and truth, connecting me to my Heavenly Father. He has shaped how I view myself, provided precepts and mental models to navigate life challenges, and helped me become the man God designed me to be. John is more than a friend, mentor, and guide. His impact goes beyond my own life. I would not be who I am today without him.

-David McMillian, CEO

Over the seventeen years I've known and learned from him, John has always infused me with courage. He has guided me through the most challenging times, personally and professionally. When I wanted to crawl into a hole and hide from life, John lifted me and gave me the courage to claim God's promises and rise above my temporary circumstances. He has helped me to find peace, love, hope, and joy beyond anything I could have imagined. My professional success since meeting with him is a fantastic addition!

-Wade Huges, CEO and Chairman

I was introduced to John through a mutual CEO friend who said, "If you ever hear me say anything wise about business, it probably came from John Richie." Now, it's my turn to say the same. I've only worked with John for seven years, but in that time, our coaching sessions have reframed my core principles on leadership, communication, and strategy. He's walked me through high-stakes negotiations and held me up through critical challenges.

John has made a lasting impact on my life. I hope he can do the same for you through this book.

I've been blessed with some exceptional mentors and advisors throughout my career. John Richie ranks among the best. John's counsel has guided me through every major decision, thorny business dilemma, and complex family matter over the years I've known him. Why? Because John is the most keenly insightful, unflinchingly courageous, and brilliantly intelligent man I know. He can listen intently, ask probing questions, and synthesize information into wise counsel. When John speaks, I listen. Most importantly, I've seen first-hand how John intentionally integrates his relationships, business practices, and thinking with his Christian faith. I heartily recommend *Courage Required*.

-Bryan Owens CEO

As my mentor and coach, John's deep-rooted faith in Jesus profoundly influences his perspective and forms the cornerstone of his guidance. His wisdom combines extensive reading and rich personal experiences, complemented by his journey alongside many of my peers. John has a unique talent for turning complex ideas into practical, transformative advice. I eagerly anticipate seeing his insights in print and can't wait to read his book, which I am confident will inspire and guide many.

-Scott Coger CEO

John has been an encourager and wise counselor. He leaks wisdom. Spend time with him or read his words. You are sure to gain. There hasn't been an interaction where I wasn't encouraged or uplifted. John's wisdom brings tough, thought-provoking questions followed by patient support in processing. He tells applicable stories from his experience. He has helped me grow in my leadership skills and become a faithful steward in business, marriage, and family, as well as with my soul.

-Miller Chalk, CEO

I have had the privilege of having John Richie as my coach for the past seventeen years. His guidance has been instrumental in helping me build a good company. Countless times, his method of listening and questioning has helped me achieve clarity in understanding problems and making decisions. John understands that my business is deeply intertwined with all aspects of my life, and his holistic approach has helped me achieve balance and growth, both professionally, personally, and spiritually.

I have witnessed firsthand how John's coaching principles have empowered many others to succeed. Any coach who applies John Richie's methods will undoubtedly make a significant impact on the individuals they guide, just as John has made on me.

–Paul McGraw, CEO

As I sat in a hotel lobby on my first day meeting John, I had no idea what would transpire in my life. My journey was unknown, but I was in for the ride. What an experience it has been so far. John has helped me and my marriage, family, and business thrive. John's divine perspective comes from his unbridled faith, experience, wisdom, and shared stories. He meets me where I am, sometimes with hard-hitting truth bombs, all delivered with grace and a hug. John has strengthened my courage to handle current and upcoming challenges as life unfolds. One thing is for sure: I'm on the right path with the help of my friend and mentor, John Richie, and his God-powered mind.

–Robbi Raitt, CEO

John has been a steady presence in my life for nearly two decades, walking alongside me through the uncertainty of post-college life, to premarital counseling, and into adulthood. I directly benefit from one of his guiding principles: life on life, over time.

When John invited me to join his Radical Mentoring group, I told him I was at a point where I did not believe spiritual growth was possible anymore. In kindness, he did not laugh out loud. In the following years, John opened his heart and life to me. He modeled that it is possible on this side of Eden to be fully known and fully loved. He introduced me to vulnerability, trust, humility, love (which I know to be a hundred percent grace and a hundred percent truth), and courage. Through John, I experienced the love of my Heavenly Father, and my life has not recovered since. I love him, and I thank God for him.

–David Wright, Attorney

Two things stand out when I think about the fifteen years that John has been my coach. The first is the clarity and objectivity needed to avoid fear- or bias-based decisions when my identity was no longer tied to my work. The second is the passion and fulfillment that comes with finding kingdom purpose in my work. These two Richie principles forever changed my trajectory and helped my company achieve tenfold growth.

-Brad Jenkins, CEO

I have had the privilege of knowing John Richie for over a decade. I have faced numerous challenging personal and business issues, and John has consistently been my sounding board. Both my family and my company have greatly benefited from his wisdom. I often wish I had documented all the advice he has shared with me. I hope John can guide you through this book as he has guided me.

-Bert Blackburn, CEO

COURAGE REQUIRED

COURAGE REQUIRED

*Reflections on the Intersection
of Faith and Leadership*

JOHN RICHIE

COURAGE REQUIRED
Reflections on the Intersection of Faith and Leadership

Copyright © 2024 by John Richie

Interior Layout and Design by Stephanie Anderson
Book Cover Design by Rachel Royer
Editorial by Cindy McCachern and Jamie Tews

ISBNs:
979-8-89165-187-6 *Paperback*
979-8-89165-188-3 *Hardback*
979-8-89165-189-0 *E-book*

Published by:
Streamline Books
Kansas City, MO
streamlinebookspublishing.com

PREFACE

OR YEARS, A raft of people have encouraged and pestered me to write a book. This book is dedicated to them. Thank you for believing, pushing, inspiring, and following my progress. Even as I started, you were interested in the project and believed in me. This book would never have happened if not for you. My wife, Martha, has long encouraged me to write.

I resisted the idea of writing a book for a few decades. I had a hard time imagining the final product and who might be interested. Writing a book is a lot of work, and other things demand my time. However, all of that began to change in late 2023.

In the last year, events came together to develop a vision for a conversational book. The one-to-one context is where I feel most comfortable. Most books are anything but conversational. The conversational vision opened the door to considering a book. In the key conversation, a dear friend said, "I want your book to sound like our conversations at Eggs Up on Thursday." This was, at last, a vision I could get my head around. Everything that exists in the visible world first existed in the invisible world. This book is no exception. It began to exist in the invisible world during our "Eggs Up" conversation.

A vision was not enough. Writing a book requires much effort and courage to transform it from the invisible world into a physical product.

To make a book possible, I needed several crucial things:

First, I had to connect to a very important group of people. I needed an advisor and editor as well as the infrastructure to advise, correct, proof, and print. The world of bringing a book to market is outside of my experience.

Second, there needed to be a process for producing a book faithful to the vision. I am certain that if the only process were me pecking away at a keyboard late into the night, we would still be waiting.

Third, the people closest to me who would bear some of the costs of writing a book needed to vocally and enthusiastically support the effort, cost, and mindshare. My wife, Martha, is at the top of that list. Her support for this project was enthusiastic and instantaneous. She was a constant source of encouragement and energy.

Then, there had to be urgency. Shakespeare wrote, "There is a tide to the affairs of men." This spring was the tide. This spring, I had the time, perspective, health, and energy to do it. I dare not presume on next spring.

Finally, dear reader, there had to be you. Without a picture of the people who would read this, it could never have been finished. I pray it will serve you in your journey.

CONTENTS

INTRODUCTION

A S I GET OLDER, I find my resume becomes less and less important in explaining who I am. For the past twenty years, I have served as an executive coach to Christian businessmen—a role that has allowed me the privilege of being deeply involved in their professional and personal lives. This book represents the culmination of my experiences, failures, and insights, and it represents the wisdom I have gathered over the years.

I live in the Atlanta area with my wife, Martha, who is far wiser than I am. We raised our three children here, and two of them now live nearby with their families. My work experience spans from roles at a Fortune 100 company to medium-sized enterprises, cold start-ups, and small businesses. My positions have ranged from financial analyst to CEO. I have quit a job, been downsized, driven a company into the ground, grown a business, and sold it profitably to a strategic buyer. I started the coaching business I currently run, and I intend to continue until the day I turn off the lights and walk away. That day will come—but not today.

My professional career seemed irrational until I began coaching. It was in this final role that all of my previous experiences became fruitful and relevant. My journey equipped me with hard-won perspectives on risk, leadership, identity, and faith in the workplace. Twenty years of coaching CEOs have only deepened those perspectives. To be clear, much of what I have learned came from difficult experiences, including failures. As Richard Rhor said, "Success has absolutely nothing, absolutely nothing to teach you spiritually after age thirty. It just feels good."[1] I agree.

As a coach, I don't have a system or program. I generally abhor both of those in this context. I have relationships over time. This is the context that provides the most value and produces the most long lasting change—relationships over time. I don't keep a social media presence. I don't have a website. I am not easy to find except through people I work with.

The inspiration for this book stems from my desire to reach out to individuals who may not have the resources to work directly with a coach. Through my years of experience, I've realized that many of the struggles faced by those I coach are universal. These challenges include understanding one's identity, integrating faith with business, discovering personal desires, building relationships, and navigating various seasons and difficulties in life.

Each chapter in this book is designed as a series of emails to men who embody these common issues. This format offers a personal touch and practical advice, aiming to feel direct and relevant to experiences.

This book is for anyone seeking personal and professional growth while remaining true to their Christian faith. It is designed as a practical guide, filled with real-life examples and actionable advice. My hope is that these pages will offer you the encouragement, wisdom, and tools you need to navigate your own journey.

I have a deep love for reading and owe a great debt to a wide range of authors who have profoundly influenced my thinking and the ideas presented here. Their insights have shaped my coaching approach and provided me with the tools to help others. Authors like Tim Keller, Os Guinness, Bill Thrall, Jeffery Marx, Tim George, Richard Rumelt, JRR Tolkein, Michael Marquat, Lawrence Ackerman, and Henry Cloud, among many others, have had a significant impact on my thinking. There is such a long list of the men and women whose ideas have influenced me, I hate to mention any by name. I have also learned much from the people that I worked with. I have been blessed to learn from both great examples and terrible ones, and all of it has been profitable.

Thank you for allowing me to be a part of your journey. Let's embark on this adventure together, discovering new heights and deeper understandings of ourselves and the world around us.

—John Richie

1

Finding Your Identity

SYNOPSIS: This group of emails is written as a follow-up to a meeting with David, a successful entrepreneur struggling with the idea of never being good enough. Through candid and introspective correspondence, David confronts the challenge of reconciling his achievements with his relentless pursuit of perfection. As he navigates the waters of self-doubt and external expectations, readers are invited to join him. Through David's struggles and revelations, we explore the universal challenge of correctly setting your identity, without which leaders struggle.

SUBJECT:
Reigniting Your Passion and Purpose

Hey David,

I hope this email finds you well. I've been reflecting on our recent conversations about having your identity caught up in your job. As I've been thinking about it, I wanted to share some thoughts about a topic that has been significant in my journey: the association of identity with work.

For the longest time, I believed my identity was inseparable from my job. I was adamant that associating my identity with my work made me a better executive, more committed, and more engaged in my work. I regarded my close association between my job and identity as a strength, not a problem. But it took the wisdom and guidance of my own coach, Mary Ellen Brantley, to help me see that allowing my identity to be wrapped up in my job was a limiter rather than a strength.

Associating my identity with my job made me defensive and unwilling to be open to other people's ideas. It meant I always had to be right, and it kept me from taking needed risks because I had so much at stake. It also caused me to be emotional at inappropriate moments.

Successes inflated my ego, while failures left me feeling utterly defeated. It was an emotional rollercoaster ride that I couldn't get off. Tim Keller said, "If our identity is in our work, rather than Christ, success will go to our heads, and failure will go to our hearts."[2] A dear friend told me that success and failure are in the same vortex. Both men were right. When work is going well, and everything you touch turns to gold, it's easy to trust your identity to your work. But those seasons of success never last. If your identity and job are tied together, you won't be able to extract your identity from your job when troubles and failures come. And they always do.

Mary Ellen helped me understand that my identity is separate from the confines of my job. She showed me that I am more than a CEO, an entrepreneur, or any other label I might claim. She taught me that healthy executives operate their business as an "it." I'm over here with my identity, and over there is the business. The business isn't me, and I'm not the business.

This understanding was pivotal to managing my last year or so at the helm of my company. There was a moment when our most profitable customer fired us, coinciding with the company being put up for sale. Standing before the board, I explained that we had lost about a third of our shareholder value

> **The business isn't me, and I'm not the business.**

and largest customer. Because I had separated my identity from the company, I could remain composed, focusing on what we should do next. As I left the meeting, one of the board members turned to another, asking about my well-being. The response was, "I think he is sad, but he is not crushed."

I like that story because it shows how much I had separated my identity from the business. Eventually, before the deal to sell the company had concluded, our biggest customer decided to return. But, when they came back, my response was not one of desperation. Instead, I laid out stringent criteria for their reinstatement. This strategic approach shielded our company's value and propelled it forward. To a significant degree, this outcome was because I never let my identity get wrapped up in whether or not a big company fired me. That was

3

irrelevant. Instead, I had a mission to take care of the business. That's what I focused on—not on me. I had plenty of not-great moments as a CEO but this was one of my best. Not having my identity wrapped up in work made me a much better executive. I could focus on the mission, not how work affected me.

> **Significance is received, not achieved.**

David, I share all this with you because I see a similar struggle in you—a struggle to break free from the chains of having your identity bound up in what you do professionally. Significance is received, not achieved. Value is established by our Heavenly Father, not by our success or failure at work. Separating work and identity will make you a better leader and a happier person. I know it's not an easy journey because courage is required to redefine your identity and relinquish the need for external validation. But I believe it's a journey worth taking, and I'm here to support you every step of the way.

Take care, my friend, and know that I'm always here for you.

Warm regards,
John

SUBJECT:
Reigniting Your Passion and Purpose

Hi David,

Your recent email's questions are incredibly thought-provoking. I appreciate the opportunity to delve deeper into this topic with you. I am so happy that you have recognized the need to disentangle yourself from your job. It's a courageous step.

I asked myself three main questions to help me separate myself from my job. These questions may also help you gain clarity and perspective. I hope they will offer you some valuable insights as well.

The first question to ask yourself is, "To whom have you given the right to judge your life?" Everyone has conferred this authority upon someone, designating them as their audience. This could be a parent, a spouse, a coach, or a boss. In my journey during my formative years, my audience was my dad. However, over time, I unknowingly transferred this authority to various male figures I encountered professionally.

Crucially, none of these men explicitly passed judgment on me. Instead, their perceived verdicts were based on my interpretation of their beliefs about me. It finally dawned on me that my Heavenly Father is the only rightful judge of my life. He alone serves as the audience for the way I live my life.

The second question revolves around significance: "Why do I matter?" The answer to this question always lies in the perceptions of our audience. Subconsciously, I believed that if those who judged me rendered favorable assessments, then I mattered. On the other hand, negative judgments led me to internalize feelings of insignificance.

My worth depended entirely on their opinions. This dynamic exerted a powerful influence, driving me to seek their approval at all costs.

However, when my Heavenly Father assumes the role of my judge, my significance and value derive from his perception of me. Consider the worth of something in terms of what someone is willing to pay. In this context, Jesus established my value on the cross, serving as the price God paid for a relationship with me. Consequently, my significance is not achieved but received—a heavy burden is lifted. I did not earn my significance, so I can't lose it either.

The third and final question brings me into focus: Who am I? Or, put another way, "What is the story I tell myself about myself?" Identity invariably flows from significance. For years, my identity was wrapped up in the opinions of powerful men. Their perception of my significance shaped my identity–if they thought highly of me, I was a winner; if not, I was a failure.

Powerful men find broken men. I have experienced this reality firsthand from both perspectives. The broken man becomes reliant on the judgment of his authority figure, striving to earn favor or facing devastation from disapproval. Manipulation comes easily to the powerful as they seek people in need of validation from external sources. However, recognizing myself as a chosen child of the living God shifted my perspective, allowing me to detach my worth from these external influences. Embracing this identity provided a stable foundation for constructing a more authentic sense of self.

Moreover, becoming a "leader of no reputation" deeply resonated with me. This concept stems from the King James translation of Philippians 2:6-7, where Paul describes Jesus as one who "did not regard equality with God a thing to be grasped" and ultimately "became a man of no reputation." This idea was profoundly counterintuitive to my belief in the importance of reputation. Eventually, I understood it as prioritizing fidelity to the mission over personal reputation, steadfastly adhering to one's calling without apology. Jesus exemplifies this mindset, directing his focus toward his mission rather than concern for others' opinions of him. When the leader allows his energy to be fully directed to the mission at hand and not to building or protecting his reputation, he will be functioning at a high level.

I sat with one of the leaders I coach and wrote these three questions on the brown paper tablecloth between us.

1 Who is your judge?
2 Why do you matter?
3 Who are you?

He looked down for a moment and then looked into my face. "I know the Sunday School answers to all three, but I have no idea of the real answers."

Finding the real answers and bringing those answers into healthy alignment is not easy and demands courage. It's a journey and requires us to confront the truth about ourselves. However, as you delve into these questions and face them head-on, you'll gradually find greater alignment and peace in your life.

Take care, David; I hope to hear from you again soon.

Warm regards,
John

SUBJECT:
Living Out of Your Greater Story

David,

Thank you for sharing your ongoing struggle with taking failure personally. Many of us face a common challenge, and I appreciate your vulnerability in discussing it.

Your question about overcoming this tendency brings to mind the concept of our greater and lesser stories, which could offer valuable insight and guidance in navigating through this difficulty. Allow me to share some thoughts on this matter.

As I've come to understand it, identity is the story we tell ourselves about ourselves, always rooted in truth. Often, people have two stories—a greater and a lesser story. A powerful example of this dichotomy can be found in the story of Moses and the Israelites.[3]

Moses, as a leader, faced the monumental task of shifting the identity of the Israelites from slaves to God's chosen people. During their four-hundred-year enslavement in Egypt, they developed an identity that they were just slaves. This identity was true, but it was their lesser story. Moses knew that they were more than just slaves. He understood their true identity lay in their origin story—a narrative of creation, fall, and eventual redemption. Through writing the book of Genesis, Moses sought to write down their origin story. He wanted to embed this greater story into the collective consciousness of the Israelites, guiding them toward a deeper understanding of their identity as God's chosen ones. It was an act of profoundly wise leadership. He could not lead a nation of slaves to create a new nation in the

Promised Land. Instead, he needed to lead people who were strong in their understanding that they were chosen by God for this purpose.

Similarly, many individuals today grapple with two distinct narratives about themselves—a greater story that speaks to their inherent worth and purpose and a lesser story characterized by self-doubt and inadequacy. You can identify your own greater and lesser story. From our discussions, I've seen that your greater story of being a successful entrepreneur and beloved child of God is often overshadowed by your lesser story of feeling like a poor boy from a small town. Despite your achievements, you seem to struggle with a deep-seated belief that you don't matter. Both stories are true, but your greater story is always "truer" than your lesser story. Though both narratives may coexist, it is ultimately your choice of which one to live out.

In moments of anxiety or failure, it's natural to revert to your lesser story. You must remember that you always have the option to embrace your greater story—the story of your identity as beloved child of God imbued with inherent worth. Living out of this greater story empowers you to transcend the limitations of your lesser narrative and embrace your true identity.

Realizing that significance is found in God brings about a profound shift because it settles the matter of significance. It's not a matter of striving to earn or achieve significance; it's about acknowledging and receiving what has already been graciously given. Your identity as a child of God is not contingent on a job title, financial status, or any external achievements. Instead, it is rooted in the unshakeable truth of being an adopted child of a living God who has been grafted into the family. Your only challenge is to receive what's already been given to you.

Once you accept this wonderful gift from God, you will realize identity is not dependent on your business or investments. It is independent of what you have or do. Instead, you are something that flows out of authority and significance. This understanding liberates you

> **If you didn't earn your significance, you can't lose it.**

from the pressure to prove yourself through worldly measures and empowers you to live authentically out of the abundance of God's love and acceptance.

David, as you grapple with taking failure personally, I encourage you to reflect on your greater story—your inherent worth and purpose as a valued individual. Though the journey may be challenging, embracing this greater narrative will ultimately lead to more alignment and peace in your life.

I hope you can find both your greater story and your lesser one. Learning to live out of your bigger and better story will change your life. Remember, if you didn't earn your significance, you can't lose it.

Take care, David, and know that I'm here to support you every step of the way.

Regards,
John

SUBJECT:
Discovering Your Purpose

Hello David,

By now you have likely figured out that I love questions. Good questions demand answers. There is something about a good question that does not allow our brain to rest until we have an answer. Questions have power because they engage the mind and heart while lowering our defenses. As you work through important issues like purpose, I hope I can help prompt you with good questions to help you reach conclusions.

Once you have settled on living out of your greater story, the next question becomes, "What is my purpose?" Purpose, I've found, is not merely a peg in the air waiting to be plucked; instead, it emerges from a deep understanding of who we are called to serve.

Before discovering our purpose, we must confront a different question: Who are my people? This introspective understanding serves as the bedrock upon which our purpose is built.

This realization dawned on me as I recognized my affinity and connection with CEOs grappling with the myriad pressures, uncertainties, and triumphs inherent in their roles. Over the past two decades, these leaders have been my people as I've walked alongside them, offering support and understanding born from shared experiences. As Scripture aptly states, the comfort we receive is the comfort we can extend to others.

Indeed, our purpose emerges from a deep understanding of our identity, audience, and significance. It is rooted in our unique story, our connection with our people, the ones we are called to serve. Our own struggles and trials usually lead us to identify our people.

A few years ago, my wife and I moved into a house that faces west. As a result, we've been blessed to see the sunset unfold before us each evening. We take turns calling the other one to come see the breathtaking beauty outside our window. It's a simple yet profound experience that has taught me much. Before this, I didn't fully grasp the unique beauty of sunsets. However, over two decades in this home, I've realized that no two sunsets are alike. Each evening brings its blend of colors, patterns, and moods, creating a breathtaking display of God's artistry.

Reflecting on these daily wonders, I've seen a striking parallel to our relationship with our Heavenly Father. Just as each sunset is uniquely beautiful, so is our connection with God. Your experience with him differs from mine, and someone else's experience differs yet again. Despite these differences, there remains a comforting consistency in knowing that the sun will set reliably and predictably each day.

Yet, it's the way we interpret and describe these sunsets that sets them apart. Similarly, our relationships with God are shaped by our perceptions, experiences, and interactions with Him. Just as every sunset is unique, so is each of our relationships with God, slightly different from that of every other person. This relationship informs our greater story, characterized by rest, confidence, and security. People will articulate their greater story differently because of their relationship with God. But the greater story always comes from a place of rest, confidence, and security. Now, you are free to act because you are not at risk. It transcends the transient narratives of our achievements or failures, anchoring us in an unshakeable truth.

At its core, leadership is about charting a course toward a destination. It involves painting a vivid picture of where we are headed, who we are becoming along the way, and who we are meant to serve. This destination must be distinctive, drawing some in while repelling others. If your destination as a leader does not repel, it will also not attract. So, the one that ends up with a mushy middle-of-the-road description of who they're going to be will never be able to create an intense and powerful team because people will not be attracted to it.

As a business leader, you must describe the mission in concrete and meaningful ways to attract people. At the same time, you must be fearless enough to craft something that repels those who don't belong. What some people find compelling will repel others. It is hard to put something out there that you know will be rejected by some. For instance, being a Navy SEAL may not appeal to everyone, but those drawn to it are fully committed.

Creating such a culture requires courage—the courage to be bold and unapologetically true to your vision, even if it means turning away those who don't align with it. Companies like Google and Chick-fil-A exemplify this courage, crafting cultures that both attract and repel. We find passionate individuals eager to contribute to a shared purpose on the edges, not in the messy middle.

David, as you continue your journey of self-discovery and leadership, remember that your purpose flows from your identity and relationship with God. Embrace the uniqueness of your story, and have the courage to lead.

With clarity and conviction,
John

2

Integrating Faith and Business

 **SYNOPSIS:** These emails are written to a business owner who is a long-time believer but has always wondered how his faith should impact his business. Throughout the years, he has observed a wide spectrum of approaches to integrating faith and business. Some individuals openly express their faith within their professional endeavors, while others maintain a strict separation between their faith and their business practices. Now at a crossroads, he seeks to discern the right path forward for his own business. Through his conversations with his coach, readers will explore the challenges and nuances of merging faith with commerce.

SUBJECT:
Integrating Faith and Business

Dear Kevin,

What does it mean to be a Christian businessman? I know that this topic weighs heavily on your mind. As a fellow believer and business owner, I understand the complexities and uncertainties of navigating these realms because I have struggled with them myself.

I have no idea if God wants you to be rich, powerful, or successful, but I am certain that God wants to conform your character to the person of Christ. This realization has been a guiding principle in my journey as a Christian entrepreneur.

I've often kept leadership and work in completely different boxes. Early in my work career, I lived a very compartmentalized life. I had faith over here in a little bucket. I had my family over here in a little bucket. I had some friends over here in a little bucket and work over there in a great big bucket. I lived in these buckets, never thinking the items in each bucket could touch each other. I never let them overlap because I was afraid of the complexity of managing my buckets if they all touched.

> **I am certain that God wants to conform your character to the person of Christ.**

As I entered my forties, I worked around some people who lived an integrated life. This was the first time I had seen something like it. At first, I was mildly offended because their work, family, faith, and friends were all jumbled up together. I was not sure what I thought about it.

16

It certainly has some temptations and some threats associated with it. But the more I watched, the more I realized how much less energy it took for these people with an integrated life. It was incredibly powerful because they were the same person in every aspect of their life and seemed to make them richer and truer. Living like that allowed their faith, family, and work to be guided and energized through the same principles.

Meeting these people began to change how I thought about faith and work. I started to bring faith to work. It was a real struggle because there was so much superficial thinking about this in Christendom. I didn't find any description of bringing faith to work that felt true.

In my experience, integrating faith into the workplace involves more than simply applying biblical principles to business practices. It's more than using business as an evangelistic platform. It's about embodying faith in every aspect of our lives and allowing our values to permeate our actions and decisions. This integrated approach may seem daunting at first, but it brings a sense of coherence to our personal and professional lives.

In essence, living out our faith in the marketplace requires us to rely on our relationship with God, the guidance of the Holy Spirit, and the support of our fellow believers. While Scripture may not provide all the answers to our business dilemmas, it directs us back to the foundational principles of love, integrity, and service. Ultimately, our goal as Christian business leaders is not merely financial success or professional acclaim but the transformation of our hearts and the lives of those around us.

Where do you find direction for living as a Christian CEO? Scripture is indeed authoritative and holds profound wisdom, but its primary purpose is not to serve as a handbook for business. While it provides invaluable guidance, its primary purpose is to tell about God and redemption.

While the Bible addresses faith, morality, and redemption, it does not offer comprehensive rules for navigating every business scenario. Scripture is sufficient because it gives us everything we need to know about life. But it is not exhaustive. It only tells us some of what there is to know.

Consider Exodus 21:25, which offers precise instructions on what to do when an ox gores a neighbor. Scripture is simply silent about modern business dilemmas like artificial intelligence, managing layoffs, or hiring a new executive.

In facing such challenges, we are pushed back to our relationship with God, the Holy Spirit, and fellow believers. These connections provide a source of wisdom and counsel, helping us navigate the complexities of the marketplace with integrity and discernment. It's why we need to build a life that is intimately connected to other believers who face the same challenges we do.

Moreover, while we may not have clear directives from Scripture on matters like financial success or career advancement, we can be certain of God's overarching desire to conform us to the image of Christ. Regardless of our ambitions or aspirations, God's ultimate agenda is to mold our character and transform us into reflections of him.

As Christians, from the janitor to the CEO, our primary task is to love our neighbor, whether we wield significant influence or minimal power. This calling to love looks different for each person and each context but is universal. While the answers to our challenges may not always be readily apparent in Scripture, our commitment to embodying Christ-like love remains steadfast.

I'm certain that God wants to use your life to conform your character to the person of Christ. Regardless of what your agenda is, that's his agenda. He's always about that process. We can see in every circumstance that's what he's interested in. He is molding you toward the person of Christ.

Kevin, are you ready to sign up for his agenda above your own? It's a big ask.

Confidently,
John

SUBJECT:
Hearing God's Guidance in Business

Hi Kevin,

I appreciate your curiosity about how God leads us in our business endeavors. It's a profound and complex topic, but one worth exploring deeply.

I've concluded that God desires to communicate with us more than we want to hear from him. His primary mode of communication is through Scripture. Yet, many people don't invest the effort to discern how God leads them. We often find ourselves preoccupied with our own agendas, seeking direction on decisions like turning left or right. In contrast, God is more concerned with how we treat others and embody his principles.

In Romans 12:1-2, Paul promises that we will know the perfect will of God if we do not conform to the patterns of this world but present our bodies as living sacrifices, allowing our minds to be renewed. Surrendering ourselves entirely enables us to perceive God's will more clearly. It's akin to signing a blank check before knowing the amount—our willingness to surrender precedes our understanding. We wish it worked the other way around and God would disclose his will to us so we can evaluate if we are willing to transform our minds and present our bodies as a living sacrifice. It just doesn't.

God speaks to us through prayer and our circumstances, but his guidance isn't akin to real-time GPS navigation. It's often principle-based and operates on a higher level. Those who diligently seek his guidance almost always receive it clearly, while those who approach less diligently usually miss out. When God communicates, he is never vague or cryptic. God is not playing a cosmic game of hide the pea, trying to get you to discover his will that he is trying to hide. Remember, he wants to communicate with you more than you want to listen. The Holy Spirit, residing within us, guides us toward God's interests, which may not always align with our own.

There is a concept known as special revelation, where God communicates directly with you through his Spirit in your mind. It's important to remember that God never provides special revelation that contradicts his written word. I work with a man who occasionally hears from God. When he believes he has received such revelation, it prompts him to search the Bible and consult mature Christians for confirmation. He believes in special revelation but approaches it with great caution.

There are moments when God calls us to action, and if we refuse, our spiritual journey will stall until we obey. We would like to pick and choose when to obey. When we don't obey, our spiritual progress is stalled. However, God is patient and willing to wait. He doesn't position himself as an indulgent parent but as an authoritative guide.

Ultimately, God's agenda for our lives is about conforming our character to the image of Christ. It's less about specific business decisions and more about embodying his love and principles in every aspect of our lives, including our work.

Let's keep talking about this topic. I don't think we are finished yet. Do you?

Warm regards,
John

SUBJECT:
Understanding God's Guidance in Business

Kevin,

Through the years, I've struggled to determine the purpose of business. I realized that Martin Luther answered that question a long time ago.[4] He stated that the overarching purpose of all of our vocations is to love our neighbor—a sentiment echoed in Ephesians 2:10. You have certainly heard that theme running through our correspondence. The essence of our businesses is to love our neighbor. That will lead you to ask, "Who is my neighbor?" The answer is simple: the person right in front of you who needs you. In my marriage, it's my wife. As a father, it's my children. As a grandfather, it's my grandchildren. In business, my neighbors are my employees, customers, suppliers, investors, and even competitors.

One of the ways we love our neighbor is through the goods and services we sell. We often focus solely on sharing the gospel and forget that making a good product and selling it at a fair price is a primary way of serving others. For example, I am quite particular about the paper I use for writing and presenting content—the people who make that paper serve me by providing something of value to me. Similarly, when you employ people, you create opportunities for families to thrive. Running a business offers a structure where people can earn a living, support their families, and contribute to their communities. We love our neighbor through provision.

Some people think that loving your neighbor just means giving money away. Most businesses love far better by running a successful

> God's intended means of provision is commerce, not charity.

business than donating to a nonprofit. God's intended means of provision is commerce, not charity. This doesn't mean we shouldn't be charitable, but throughout history the primary means by which people provide for their lives is commerce, not the gift of a charity or a payment from a government. Provision is the legitimate function of a business.

In the 1990s and early 2000s, about a billion-and-a-half people were lifted out of absolute poverty into a middle-class lifestyle, not through government programs or charity but because of commerce.[5] People across India, China, Southeast Asia, and even parts of Africa moved from poverty to a better life because of business.

Business leaders need to recognize that they love well through commerce. If you take labor, capital, raw materials, electricity, and rent and turn them into something worth less than the sum of the inputs, you're destroying value. That's terrible stewardship. But if you can take these inputs and create something more valuable, you make a profit and you love people by provision. Building a great workplace is a vital act of loving your neighbor.

You fulfill your purpose when you create commerce and provide places for people to work. Sometimes, I feel like putting up a sign that says, "God's intended means of provision is commerce, not charity. Change my mind." This is the vocational calling of business people at a fundamental level.

Best regards,
John

SUBJECT:
Integrating Faith and Leadership

Hi Kevin,

Reflecting on our recent conversation, I am sharing a little more about integrating faith and leadership into our business lives.

A few years ago, I encountered an idea from the Danish theologian Soren Kirkegaard. His description of the three selves significantly impacted my understanding of identity and motivation. He posited that everyone has a concrete self, a best self, and a true self. The concrete self is the one we can describe with facts.[6] For example, my son is an attorney in his forties, married with three kids. This is his concrete self.

On the other hand, the best self is always a bit better than our current self—Kevin 2.0—a little kinder, thinner, more innovative, or more successful. We haven't yet achieved it, much like a new and improved version of ourselves. This best self is an aspiration but still within what we perceive as possible.

Kierkegaard's third idea, the true self, is the self entirely at rest in God's love. This got me thinking: How would I behave if I were entirely at rest in God's love? What would motivate me? For most of my life, fear and greed have been reliable motivators. But if those were removed, what would drive me? Initially, it seemed wonderful to be peaceful, like floating in the ocean. But then I questioned, would I just become inert if I didn't have fear and greed to drive my motivations? That thought was troubling.

After thinking about it, I concluded that I would have nothing to gain or lose if I were truly at rest in God's love. This state would allow me to be motivated solely by love and thankfulness. These are powerful motivators, far surpassing the small ball levers of fear and greed. While fear and greed might help accomplish some things, achieving great things requires the vast motivators of love and thankfulness.

Paul said he had learned to be content in all circumstances, whether having little or plenty (Philippians 4:11-13, NIV). Being perfectly at rest in God's love means I don't fear losing anything or having to grasp for more. I already have all I need, allowing me to operate in complete freedom. The freest person in the world is perfectly at rest in God's love.

The 23rd Psalm begins with "The LORD is my shepherd" (Psalm 23:1-6, KJV). Notice that "LORD" is written in all capitals, indicating that it refers to the holy name of God in Hebrew. Referring to God by this name was the most exalted way the psalmist could address Him.

Essentially, the holy and almighty God of the universe has chosen to be my personal shepherd. When understood this way, the phrase "I shall not want" transforms into "what else could I want?"

Being completely at rest in God's love in the practical world can be a struggle, like trying to align two magnets that push against each other. However, we can experience seasons where it is true, where we are more at rest in God's love. The Christian life is always a process—an ocean to swim in, not a mountain to climb. It isn't about reaching perfection but about learning to live at peace, surrounded by God's love.

A *New York Times* bestselling author tells a powerful story about his mother who escaped Iran after becoming a Christian.[7] When she found her way to America, someone asked why she left her rich and comfortable life in Iran. Why would she leave the home her family had lived in for generations? Her answer was profound: "Because it's true."

This woman's answer strikes at the heart of the matter. Either the gospel is true, or it's not. When faced with difficult circumstances, we must grapple with this question. If you conclude that Christianity is true, everything else aligns accordingly. If it's not, then you're on your own. For her, the decision wasn't economic, political, or philosophical but immensely practical.

Jesus compared the kingdom of God to a treasure hidden in a field for which a wise man would sell everything he had to obtain (Matthew 13:44, NIV). Paul similarly noted that if Christ has not been raised, we are most likely to be pitied (1 Corinthians 15:19, NIV). But if it is true, everything about faith and leadership falls into place. It clears away obstructions and cultural baggage because it is the ultimate truth.

Kevin, I know that believing the gospel's truth will change you. Can you imagine living out your true self, completely at rest in God's love? What would be different? I can't wait to see what happens.

Best regards,
John

SUBJECT:
A Story of Service and Impact

Hi Kevin,

In response to your recent question about integrating faith and business life, I wanted to share the story of a close friend who beautifully exemplifies this principle. My friend was going through a challenging period in his company. A private equity firm had bought the controlling interest in his business, effectively sidelining him. While in this professional exile, he discovered a profound need in Africa amidst the AIDS epidemic. The problem was stark: when a man died, his family would often take all his possessions, leaving his wife and children destitute. The only means for these widows to survive was usually through prostitution.

My friend came up with the innovative idea of starting a transcription business in Zambia. I was privileged to be a small part of the conversation that led him to this insight. Together, we realized that the purpose of business is to serve one's neighbor. He found his neighbors in these vulnerable women in Zambia. I distinctly remember him saying, "My business grows in proportion to what Zambia needs." That statement left a lasting impression on me.

Our Venture Group rallied, raising the necessary funds to start the business. It was a significant project involving setting up an internet connection where the internet did not exist, finding a building, hiring security, and providing training. Sometimes, we had to teach the women to read before they could learn to type. Identifying the women who could thrive in this new role was challenging.

Today, there are 140 workstations in Zambia, and hundreds of women have gone through the program. They have learned valuable skills, making them highly sought after in the job market. This initiative not only provided them with employment but also transformed their lives.

However, this endeavor presented other challenges. We discovered that these women had no safe place to keep their money. Many hid their earnings in their mattresses, which made them vulnerable to theft. So, we helped them set up essential banking solutions to protect their savings. Additionally, we found that many women did not leave their work stations during lunch breaks because they didn't have food to eat. We addressed this by providing meals at the worksite.

This project was connected to a Christian school in Zambia, and the profits from the transcription business now cover about sixty percent of the school's costs. It's been a remarkable journey, demonstrating how faith can drive impactful business solutions.

But is this the blueprint for every Christian business? I don't think so. This was a unique answer for us; only some are called to create a company in Zambia. However, everyone can embrace the principle that the purpose of business is to love your neighbor.

> "
> **Integrating faith into your business requires courage.**

Integrating faith into your business requires courage and doesn't always look the same for everyone. It's about finding ways to serve and love those around you through your work. This story of my friend is one example of how that can look, but your path may be different. The key is to seek God's guidance and be open to how he wants to use your business to make a difference.

Can you imagine having a business purpose like the one in this story? What would that require from you?

Best regards,
John

3

Discovering Your Heart's Desires

 **SYNOPSIS:** A conversation with Andy, a businessman in his mid-forties who grew up in the wheatfields of Nebraska but pursued his education at Duke University. Despite his humble beginnings, Andy was always driven by a desire for the latest and greatest things, constantly seeking bigger, faster, and better. He was bombarded with societal messages telling him what he should want, which led to a continuous cycle of wanting more.

Amidst this noise, Andy learned the importance of retreating to a quiet place to listen to God. Every few months, he would take several days away by himself, seeking clarity and direction. During these times of solitude, he discovered a profound understanding of his true desires, not the loud wants but the deeper, more meaningful aspirations.

SUBJECT:
Discovering Your True Desires

Dear Andy,

It was so good to talk with you recently. I've been reflecting on our recent conversations about understanding the desires of your heart. I wanted to share some thoughts that might help you on this journey.

Desire drives people more than anything else. From childhood to adulthood, so much of what we do every day is motivated by something we want. It's a fundamental part of being human. One of the key challenges we face is distinguishing between what we want most and what we want right now. As we mature, it becomes increasingly important to focus on our deeper, long-term desires rather than our immediate, seemingly urgent ones.

Desire can be a complex and sometimes misleading guide. It's often mimetic—a term derived from "mime"—meaning we want something because we see others enjoying it. This phenomenon explains why you might suddenly want a Tesla after your neighbor gets one. Many of our desires aren't our own; those around us shape them. Fashion, trends, and social norms often drive us to want what others have. This mimetic desire makes it challenging to discern what we genuinely want versus what we think we should want.

We have two kinds of desires: loud desires and deep desires. Loud desires are the immediate wants that are easily satiated. In contrast, deep desires lie beneath the surface. They require quiet reflection to uncover. These are the desires that truly matter—the desire to belong, to be loved, to know and be known, to serve, and to connect with others and with God. When God says he wants to give us the desires of our hearts, he's speaking to these deep, genuine desires, not the louder ones.

One of the fundamental truths I've learned from Ecclesiastes is that God doesn't allow us to use things he intended for our satisfaction as sources of ultimate fulfillment. He gives us good gifts that make our lives rich and satisfying. Relationships, family, and titles are gifts for our pleasure, not the core of our significance. They bring joy but not the profound fulfillment our hearts crave.

Our deepest desires are placed within us by God—to serve him and to connect with him. As David expresses in the 23rd Psalm, "Surely goodness and mercy have followed me all the days of my life, and I will dwell in the house of the Lord forever" (Psalm 23:6, KJV). This speaks to a deep, enduring desire to be with God, a desire that has pursued us throughout our lives.

Ultimately, our connection with God is our most profound and satisfying desire. Deep desires revolve around love, connection, service, and making a difference in the lives of others. These are the desires that consistently bring true satisfaction. The temporary pleasures of owning new things or seeking applause may give a fleeting thrill, but they cannot fill the deeper void within us.

What would it take for you to find the time to get away from the noise and demands of your life to listen to God? Do you believe he would help you understand your deepest desires?

I am looking forward to hearing your thoughts.

John

SUBJECT:
Defining Success through Deep Desires

Hi Andy,

I hope you're doing well. I appreciate your thoughtful question about measuring success. It's a profound and important inquiry that we all wrestle with at some point.

As we navigate our lives and desires, we often encounter the concepts of "for" and "from." Are we seeking for love or are we seeking from love? The distinction is transformative. When we seek belonging from love, we start from a foundation of already possessing these things. We rest in God's love and operate from that secure place.

I took a sabbatical to the beach a couple of years ago to think about some of these questions. I made a long list of what I wanted. But as I examined my list, I realized that everything on it was driven by loud desires stemming from my lesser identity rather than my greater identity as God's chosen child. It was a wake-up call. True fulfillment comes from our deeper desires, not the wants screaming for our attention.

Success is about pursuing what we want most, not what we want right now. A sixteen-year-old might have a long list of immediate wants, but success lies in deferring those for deeper, more meaningful desires. It's almost impossible for a sixteen-year-old to be that mature, and that's alright. We should not expect a sixteen-year-old to act out of the hard-won maturity of a fifty year old.

God says he longs to give us the desires of our hearts, but he's referring to our deep desires, not the loud ones like a new car or a beach house. He is not a device to satisfy our loud desires; he is the answer to our deepest ones. Our deep desires align with the good works for which God created us, as mentioned in Ephesians 2:10. These desires are always oriented toward serving others and fulfilling our relational needs, especially our relationship with God.

> **He is not a device to satisfy our loud desires; he is the answer to our deepest ones.**

To identify our deepest desires, we must reflect on what satisfies us. While Scripture guides us, our deep desires are seldom about applause, approval, power, comfort, or ease. They are about service, love, and connection.

I carry a quote: "We are defined not by what we want from life but by what life wants from us."[8] Life places demands on us. Our desires are important, but they are not always the most important thing. Life places demands on us often as a surprise. Unbidden, we face the needs of a parent's failing health or a child's special needs or a business crisis. How you respond can be life defining.

My father and mother had highly traditional gender roles in their marriage. My mom took care of dad. But when she got Alzheimer's, an unexpected life demand, my father rose to the occasion. I fondly remember them at the nursing home. My dad fed mom every meal, brushed her teeth and prayed with her, long after she forgot who he was. My dad's role was defined by what his life required of him in its most difficult moments.

In his book *Don't Waste Your Life*, John Piper shares a poignant story about a couple who spent their lives collecting shells after retiring.[9] Piper challenges us to imagine standing before the Lord and presenting our shells as the sum of our life's work. It's a stark reminder that God gives us freedom and autonomy to make a difference, not just to collect shells.

Clayton Christensen, a professor of innovation at Harvard Business School, arrived at a similar conclusion. In his article *How Do You Measure Your Life?*, Christensen reflected that "doing deals does not yield the deep rewards that come from building up people."[10] Coincidentally, many people remember Christensen because his influential work *The Innovator's Dilemma* was the only book on Steve Jobs' bookshelf.[11]

How you define success is central, Andy. It's a personal question. Is success for you about accumulating money, possessions, and status, or is it about aligning your life with your deepest desires rooted in service, love, and connection? Ultimately, it's about living out the good works God has prepared for you and finding fulfillment in those pursuits. May you discover the deepest desires of your heart.

Truth and Grace,
John

SUBJECT:
The Defining Clarity of Purpose

Hi Andy,

Thanks for your thoughtful question about setting priorities in life. It's a crucial aspect of leadership, faith, and identity.

Clarity of purpose always circles back to knowing your identity and audience—people who only focus on the urgent end up managing tasks but miss out on real success. Clarity of purpose does not just tell us what to pursue in the coming years but what to do this week.

I recently spoke with a guy who is considering selling his company. This brought him face-to-face with the fact that his identity is deeply tied to being the CEO. He was uncomfortable becoming part of a bigger business because his sense of significance was tied to his current role. His struggle is common—significance is seen as something to be achieved rather than received.

When we understand our significance as received—rooted in our identity as God's children—we are liberated from the need to rely on external accomplishments for our self-worth. This shift allows us to embrace our God-given identity and follow God's direction for our life more freely and authentically.

We all have a purpose, and God leaves us here to fulfill it. The key to discovering your purpose lies in identifying your people—the ones to whom God has called you. Once you have a clear understanding of your identity, the next step is to find those people. Purpose flows from people.

If you pay attention, you will notice that this is the first of my questions that is externally oriented. Questions like "Who is my audience?" or "Why do I matter?" are internal and focus on you. However, asking "Who are my people?" takes you beyond yourself and directs your attention to others.

The key to discovering your purpose lies in identifying your people.

God has placed the people in your life for you to love and serve. People often connect with groups with whom they understand or share experiences. For instance, I have a dear friend, a passionate kindergarten teacher, who is drawn to young children. A family that lost a child to a drunk driver may develop a heart for other families in similar situations because they understand that unique pain and want to offer comfort.

Sometimes, discovering your purpose happens in unexpected, even miraculous ways. I know a missionary family who felt a profound connection to people in remote and challenging areas long before they physically arrived. The wife shared with me her affinity for the people in the North Caucasus. When I looked it up, I realized she was referring to Chechnya, perhaps one of the most difficult regions on earth! This deep-seated love for the people came before their calling to serve there.

Following that direction can help you discern your life's purpose. We are rarely given the whole picture; instead, we are given the next step. You take that step and see if it aligns with what you should do. If it doesn't, you adjust. This process involves experimentation and can lead to the realization of your calling.

In addition, we are not called to one thing forever. Our purpose can evolve, leading us to new people and callings. The discovery of purpose is often revealed through experience and experimentation. Rather than sitting in a corner trying to decide your purpose, engage in life, try different things, and see what resonates with you. Your purpose will become more apparent as you identify and serve those to whom God has called you.

Take care, Andy. I'm looking forward to hearing how your journey unfolds.

Courageously,
John

SUBJECT:
My Journey to Discover Purpose

Hi Andy,

I'm glad you're asking these deep questions about life's purpose. I've spent much of my life grappling with these very questions.

In my twenties, thirties, and even into my forties, I often asked, "Why am I here?" I longed for something that would make my life make sense and bring me God's blessing, hoping it would make my life easier and better. I changed jobs frequently, thinking that finding work that mattered to people would give my life purpose. But that approach didn't work as well as I hoped.

I vividly remember moving to Marietta, GA, and meeting with the pastor at our new church. During our first meeting, I talked about my search for purpose. I can only imagine him rolling his eyes, thinking, "Here's another thirty-something looking for purpose." It is a common struggle.

Another major challenge I faced was finding a sense of significance. Why do I matter? In my late thirties, I finally realized that I matter because God says I matter. My significance is received, not achieved.

For most of my life, I considered myself an introvert, emotionally distant, and somewhat disconnected from people. But in the past few years, I discovered that I'm intuitive and insightful about what's happening with people.

In my late forties and early fifties, I started talking to people who were in between jobs.

I matter because

God says I matter.

This endeavor evolved into a ministry for me. Over time, I spoke with between five hundred and a thousand people, listening to their stories and offering them guidance. These conversations taught me to listen deeply and empathize with the struggles of others. I became pretty good at it. While many people sought job leads, I often found myself guiding them toward discovering their purpose.

Through these interactions, I realized I had a calling to help people who were out of work. It became clear that I cared deeply for these individuals. This experience opened doors for meaningful conversations about purpose, choices, priorities, and courage. It taught me the value of curiosity, listening, and sometimes asking uncomfortable questions. I had a lot to learn.

A pivotal moment came when my friend Carl and I worked with a man going through severe marriage problems. Carl asked very personal and private questions that needed to be asked. Watching Carl's approach, I learned the importance of stepping outside my comfort zone to ask more probing and personal questions. I had always kept boundaries that precluded asking a question that would be uncomfortable. Carl gave me permission to find the courage to ask the questions that needed to be asked, uncomfortable or not.

In my fifties, I understood that relationships are the fuel of life. My conversations with people out of work helped me realize my calling to others, not just to my job. Running a business gave me empathy for business leaders and helped me understand their pressures and challenges.

I transitioned into a job that had me coaching business owners. It was perfect for me because I understood and cared about their problems. By then, I had developed good questioning skills, empathy, and genuine care for these people. My coaching skills evolved naturally, and I realized I had been preparing for this for a decade.

When I sit down with an executive, I often hear fear and anxiety in their voice. They face unique problems, and no one understands the challenges and pressures they face. Leaders frequently find themselves incredibly lonely without anyone who truly comprehends their struggles. Loneliness makes finding needed courage harder.

Through this journey, I began to understand my deepest desires. Early in my career, I had eighteen different roles in twenty-three years. Despite frequent promotions and job changes, my career only made sense when viewed in the context of what I do today as a coach. All those experiences dovetailed into my current role.

So, I've worked as a coach for the past twenty years, serving the people God had always prepared me to serve. Your purpose is usually other-centered. Life is about how we treat people. The Christian life is other-centered, focusing on how we treat one another in the community.

I hope my story might help you discover your people. To whom has God called you? Discovering the answer to that question can make all the difference.

In his service,
John

4

Understanding How People Change

SYNOPSIS: A conversation with Brent, a forty-year-old business owner who feels trapped by his past and believes he has limited choices in life. Despite his belief that he is a prisoner of his circumstances, Brent fails to recognize the power of his own agency. At forty, he still has the ability to make significant changes in both his business and personal life if he can embrace his freedom and take ownership of his decisions.

SUBJECT:
Finding Clarity and Direction in Life

Hi Brent,

I hope this email finds you well. I've been reflecting on our recent conversations. You've mentioned feeling stuck on a conveyor belt, doing the same thing over and over again.

It sounds like you're feeling quite passive in your life right now. You have a good marriage, great kids, and a stable job, yet there's this underlying unhappiness that you can't quite pin down. It seems like you've been letting life take you wherever it wants, rather than actively steering it in the direction you truly desire. This sense of passivity can be incredibly frustrating and draining.

You've mentioned your love of the ocean. So, let's engage in a bit of fantasy thinking for a moment. Imagine selling everything, moving to the Florida Keys, and buying a charter boat. Picture yourself spending your days taking people out for fishing trips, enjoying the sun, sea, and salt air. It sounds intriguing, doesn't it? Now, let's take that a step further. How do you think your wife and children would feel about this drastic change? Do you want to go without them? Would you be better off going it alone?

I'm anxious to hear your thoughts. Do you see the Keys in your future?

John

SUBJECT:
Embracing Your True Desires and Moving Forward

Hi Brent,

Thanks for your response. I'm glad you found this exercise fun and revealing. It's enlightening to see that, even in a fantasy scenario, your wife and kids remain the best part of your life. That's a powerful realization and a testament to what matters to you.

Knowing what you don't want is a crucial step in understanding what you do want. Since moving to Florida and leaving your family behind isn't what you desire, let's focus on how you can channel that clarity into creating a fulfilling life right where you are.

Being in your forties is actually a great time to make significant changes in your life. It's a period where you have enough experience to know what works and enough time to implement and enjoy new directions. It's an ideal moment to take control and make positive changes.

Change doesn't always have to be monumental. It can start with something small. For instance, you mentioned feeling out of shape. What if you started going to the gym? It might seem minor compared to the larger issues you're facing, but sometimes the smallest change can have the biggest impact.

By deciding to go to the gym, you're taking control of one aspect of your life. It's a statement that you have the power to make changes. This small shift can build momentum and help you realize that you can make other changes too. Over time, you might find the courage to have different kinds of conversations with your wife and children. It might also help you see your work as a calling rather than a prison.

Let's get practical about it. What can you do to make the change to begin going to the gym? Consider packing your gym clothes the night before and putting them in the car. This way, you eliminate any excuse not to go. Making it easy for yourself to follow through on your intention is key.

Remember, it all begins with one small change. Somewhere along the way, I began calling this first small change a dominion key. It's the first decision that allows you to exercise dominion over a part of your life. It's a key because it unlocks other changes too. Once you discover you have the power to change, you'll start using it in other areas of your life. You might also learn to think about, prepare for, and engage constructively in conflict. You have the ability to grow and develop, to take the initiative and steer your life in the direction you truly want.

Keep me posted on how your journey at the gym is going. The hard part is the first trip.

Best,
John

SUBJECT:
Understanding the Path to Change

Hi Brent,

I'm glad to hear that you've started going to the gym. Even if it feels uncertain right now, taking that first step is courageous. You've asked about how people change, so let's delve into that.

For those who started a company, it wouldn't exist without them. Yet, the company's most difficult problems all have their roots in the leader. Essentially, a company can't grow past the leader. So, in order for your company to grow, you must also grow. This necessity will put you on a path toward doing things that are unknown and challenging.

Change is inherently difficult for most people, but some manage to make significant changes. How do they do it? People change in one of three ways:

> **A company can't grow past the leader.**

First, they embrace change voluntarily. They are open to feedback and actively consider how they could adapt to meet evolving demands. This is the least costly way to change. This group is most likely to hire a coach to help them anticipate and navigate necessary changes.

The second way that people change is through pattern recognition. They realize that repeating the same actions yields the same outcome. This often painful recognition motivates them to embrace change.

Finally, some people change when reality hits them in the head. They can no longer pretend, and must confront their circumstances head-on. As you might imagine, this is the most costly and difficult path, as they must change while dealing with the consequences of their choices. As my friend Regi said, "You can't believe your way out of a problem you acted your way into."

Our development in life is like building an interstate highway. Looking back, you see the bridges built, asphalt laid, and exits installed. Looking forward, you see the swamps that need draining, the hills that need grading, and the bridges that need building. Both perspectives are equally valid—one reflects the past, the other the future. Focusing only on one direction gives an incomplete and therefore inaccurate picture. Only looking forward can leave you feeling discouraged and overwhelmed, while looking back can make you self-satisfied and over confident. As I get older, I see that I have come a long way, and I have a long way to go.

Change is usually progressive. We use the word "growth" for a reason. "Maturing" is another good term for it. Maturation doesn't happen suddenly; it generally happens slowly, over time. If we ask people to draw a line on a piece of paper and mark all the positive and negative moments of their life—the things that formed them and made them who they are—most will have been formed by the negative moments in their life, not by moments of triumph or success.

Since your company can't grow past you, you have to go first.

Truth and Grace,
John

SUBJECT:
Embracing Change and Leading Your Business Forward

Hi Brent,

I'm thrilled to hear that you've been consistently going to the gym and have already lost seven pounds! That's fantastic progress. Your commitment to making changes in your personal life is inspiring, and it's a solid foundation for addressing your questions about growing and changing with your business.

One key skill that all high-performing individuals have is the ability to play their life forward as a video.[12] They ask themselves, "If I don't do anything, what will happen in three or five years?" Envisioning the future in concrete terms catalyzes change because they're either drawn to a positive outcome or repelled by a negative one. For instance, if your relationship with your spouse continues as it is, you might become strangers in five years. If your children keep on their current path, they might end up in opposition to each other. Similarly, if your company continues as it is, it might struggle because it will have outgrown your ability to lead it. The enemy here is complacency. Just because the dragon next door did not eat you today, it does not mean it won't eat you tomorrow. It's still a dragon.

Understanding this concept is crucial. If you can play the video forward and see where your current actions will lead you, you can decide if that's the future you want. If it isn't, you can start making changes now to alter that trajectory.

Many so-called weaknesses in life are actually just preferences you don't want to give up. Progress begins with knowing where you really are and being truthful about it—not where you hope to be or where you think you should be. It's essential to ask yourself, "Where am I really?" and then play the video forward.

For example, I once worked for an organization where I had to ask myself what would happen in three years if nothing changed. The realization was stark: I wouldn't be working there. This led to a series of direct conversations and ultimately a decision to leave. Playing the video forward gave me clarity about a future crisis long before it arrived.

If you make bad decisions now, you'll have fewer options later. It's just how the world works. Poor choices lead to constrained future choices, whether in business or life. For instance, making poor strategic decisions might leave you with only one option: selling your company at a deep discount.

It's important to articulate what you want, not just what you don't want. Saying "I don't want to be a cog in a corporate machine" provides energy but no direction. I hear people making strong definitive statements about what they don't want, and they think they have been very clear. Knowing what you don't want is a small part of a solution. Instead, determine what you do want. For example, realizing I wanted to be an executive coach gave me a clear path forward.

The outcomes in your business and life result from your choices. To change the outcome, you must disrupt the existing machine. You are a finely tuned machine to get the results you're getting. If you want different results, you need to make different choices.

Remember, you're not a prisoner of your choices. We all have the ability to act and choose. If you want to make a change, you must claim that ability. You can go faster, slower, right, or left. There are countless choices, but you must be willing to make them.

Does the idea of your power to choose exhilarate you or does it give you a little pause?

All the best,
John

SUBJECT:
The Power of a Mirror

Hi Brent,

I'm thrilled to hear about your progress at the gym and your commitment to taking your company to the next level. Losing eleven pounds is a significant achievement. Making this change is a big step, and I understand it can seem overwhelming at times. Let's discuss how you can find the courage and clarity needed to move forward.

We often find courage to change when we're out of options and feeling the heat. But, we also find courage in an environment of love and acceptance, where people believe in us and encourage us in the right direction.

When we're feeling stuck, the answer isn't always found by looking inward. Introspection doesn't always get us unstuck. Few people can look inward to find the answer. They need feedback, an external point-of-view, to understand what to do. They also have to believe in their ability to change. They must imagine a future state that can exist. Everything that exists in the visible world began in the invisible world. So, if you can't imagine this future state in your head, you're not going to be able to achieve it.

The beginning of all growth is recognizing where we are right now—not where we wish we were, not where we think we are, not where we pretend to be. To see this truth, we need a mirror.

For much of my life, I kept the mirror away. I didn't get much feedback because I thought it was threatening and negative instead of liberating and positive. But today, I am much more likely to seek feedback.

When I talk about blind spots, most people think of defects—negative things we don't know about. Much more often, blind spots are positive aspects of yourself that you don't see accurately. Most people have positive attributes they don't fully understand.

I worked with a man for several years who saw himself as a blue-collar CEO. He worked hard, kept his nose clean, and moved the company ahead. He was very limited in how he saw himself. The truth was that he was incredibly good at building trusting relationships with both customers and senior executives. He created fifty million dollars in shareholder value through these relationships, but he couldn't see that his greatest gift was relational. To grow, he needed a mirror so he could begin to see himself in a relational mode. The beginning of all growth is to see yourself accurately.

To find a mirror to illuminate your path, you must ask people for help. Seeking help requires humility. A few years ago, I asked three or four friends how they experienced me. Most of the feedback was positive, but one thing I learned was that I am often unnecessarily contentious. It was true and good for me to see myself in this light. Without their help, I wouldn't have seen this about myself.

Sometimes people hire a coach to serve as a mirror, reflecting back what they see. The people in your life that can help you are not safe, and the people who are safe often can't help you. An outside, safe perspective is necessary. To be sure, there is often no one more committed to helping you see yourself clearly than your spouse. Asking for their feedback requires courage, especially when it comes to identifying what is working and what isn't. But there are business issues that many spouses can't help you with. Your friends in a small group might be safe but they have no concept of the issues you face.

Are you up for discovering the power of a mirror in your life? Does it seem intimidating or exciting? I'm here to help either way.

Truth and Grace,
John

SUBJECT:
Embracing the Cycle of Change

Hi Brent,

I'm glad to hear about your continued progress at the gym and the clarity you're gaining about what you want for your company. As you move forward on this journey, I want to share with you a framework that has been instrumental in my own growth—understanding and embracing the cycle of change.

Change follows a cycle of execution, doldrums, cocooning, and planning.[13] I use a model of a little circle to illustrate this. Our brain cycles through periods of execution, rest, frustration, and renewal. It's how God made our brains work. We have to learn to work with this cycle instead of against it.

I'll begin with execution. When I'm in the execution phase, I'm actively engaged in tasks and seeing positive results. But then, after a while, everything slows down. The things I was executing have come into place and are working (or not). I start to feel flat. Execution gives way to the doldrums.

The word "doldrums" is a sailing term for a part of the ocean where there's no wind. All the success I was experiencing has now slowed down, leaving me frustrated. Things aren't working as smoothly as they once did. Sailing captains would often put their longboats over the side of the ship and the men would try to tow the boat out of the doldrums and into the wind. I can't imagine a more miserable job!

I made a set of bets on the future, and most of them paid off. It was exciting to see the risks we took come to fruition. However, as time passes, you may begin to miss that initial exhilaration. You start to notice things about the business that are not right and become concerned about certain trends in the market. This marks the beginning of a period of developing dissatisfaction, the doldrums.

Eventually, I enter the quiet phase of cocooning. While this phase may seem inactive, it is anything but. The work done here is internal—a metamorphosis where needed inward changes are made to prepare for the coming outward transformations. You might notice I changed to the passive voice since the cocooning work happens within you but not necessarily by you. Perhaps your subconscious mind is at work, but you won't experience it that way.

Next, I move into the planning phase, laying the groundwork and action steps necessary to turn my new dream into reality. This phase is characterized by excitement and extensive planning. Once the planning is complete, I begin executing the changes I envisioned. The cycle comes full circle.

As far as I can tell, this cycle is inevitable and necessary. Each step in the cycle is essential to the outcome. The doldrums or the cocooning are not to be minimized or rushed through. There are no shortcuts.

I used to try to find ways to short-circuit the cycle. I thought I could bypass the cocooning and doldrums phases because they seemed unproductive. My approach was to simply plan and execute, over and over. But I found that it doesn't work that way. You can't skip these phases. You need these times of frustration and apparent quiet to prepare for what comes next. All leaders do.

Occasionally, I've taken a sabbatical—a period away to reflect and reimagine my direction. I find this time to be incredibly helpful. In the summer of 2021, I took a month off and spent most of it at the beach. During that time, I was "playing the movie forward."

Before I started, I gathered feedback and wrote out a set of questions I wanted to work through. The sabbatical served as my cocooning phase, during which I delved deep into myself. From an outside perspective, it might have been difficult to gauge my progress, but I spent a lot of time journaling. Once this phase concluded, I transitioned into the planning stage and soon began executing my plans. This cyclical process has proven to be highly effective for me.

Most people enter this cycle involuntarily, but once they recognize it for what it is, they can embrace it. They no longer have to fight it. Most of the time, people don't consciously decide to enter the cocooning phase—it just happens. But once the cycle begins, it becomes an integral part of how we change.

Embracing this cycle can help you navigate the changes needed to take your company to the next level. Understanding and accepting the different phases will give you the patience needed to work with our natural cycle instead of fighting it.

Can you find a time when you were in this development cycle? What did you learn?

Warm regards,
John

SUBJECT:
You Found Your Dominion Key!

Hi Brent,

Congratulations on your twenty pound weight loss! Seeing you come alive through this process is inspiring. Going to the gym turned out to be your dominion key, demonstrating that you have control over your life. Once you realized that, you expanded your agency over other aspects. The key was to start engaging. Once you started, you felt your own strength instead of weakness.

As soon as someone is convinced they have the ability to act, it will make a difference. You don't need to go to the gym every day. But if you go four days a week, more often than not, you'll change. It's easy to get discouraged by aiming for perfection and then not being able to achieve it. All you have to do is succeed more often than not.

What drives people to do what they do? Neurologist Sigmund Freud said people are driven by pleasure.[14] Philosopher Friedrich Nietzsche said we are driven by will to power.[15] But psychiatrist Viktor Frankl, in his book *Man's Search for Meaning*, contends that people are driven by meaning.[16] He explains that no one can take away our ability to respond inwardly to circumstances. The person who finds meaning inwardly has exerted dominion. If my dominion is only over what I think, I still have exerted dominion and therefore my life has meaning. While I'm careful not to reduce anything too far, I believe Frankl's explanation is closer to the truth than that of Freud or Nietzsche.

Surrounding yourself with supportive and growth-oriented people can further accelerate that process of growth and change. Motivational speaker Jim Rohn says we are the average of the five people we spend the most time with.[17] While that is not perfectly true, it is still a great insight. We are heavily influenced by the people we spend time with. When we are with curious people that are growing, engaging, and challenging themselves, we become interested in growing. Likewise, if we surround ourselves with others who do not want to change, we will find ourselves doing likewise.

It's crucial to surround yourself with the right people on your journey. My closest friends are all passionate about learning and growing; they're curious and constantly seeking challenges. I find it difficult to form deep connections with individuals who don't share these values. Almost invariably, my closest friends are those who are dedicated to personal growth, focusing more on purpose than pastimes. While we enjoy having fun, our primary drive is not leisure. There's also a unique chemistry and positive draw among us that's hard to replicate.

If you want to have change in your life, develop relationships with friends who are doing the things you want to do. For instance, I have a friend in his fifties who wanted to become more active, so he became more connected to friends who were mountain bikers.

Your dominion key is the beginning, not the end. Now that you have used your agency and taken action to make a change, it's important to remember that the purpose of this dominion key is to be used. What is the next area of your life where you need to exert some control?

Let's get going.

Truth and Grace,
John

SUBJECT:
The Power of God to Change Us

Hi Brent,

I understand how discouraging it can be when progress seems slow. It's natural to feel impatient and worry about not making changes quickly enough. However, I want to encourage you to trust in the process.

The Bible describes the gospel as the power of God for us to change. But where is this power, and what does it mean? Can we really find this power? The word the Bible uses for this power is "dynamis." It is the same word from which we get the word "dynamite." This power is transformative and explosive in its potential.

In the immaturity of my early years, I didn't see God's power to change because I was not looking for change over a long enough period. I was trying to see the power by looking at a single point in time. At any given moment, I was struggling. But, the longer I considered, I could find growth. We're made to have a growth mindset, convinced that we are not stuck and that we can do more.

Change is

often slower

than we'd like.

Change is often slower than we'd like. It can feel frustrating, but remember that true transformation takes time. You're already making progress by taking control of your life and going to the gym. Each small step forward builds on the previous one, creating a foundation for lasting change.

I am in my seventies. I'm not stuck. I have lots of growth ahead. I have less time ahead of me than I used to, but that doesn't mean I don't have growth ahead. You, too, have tremendous potential for growth and change.

To tap into this power, it's crucial to have a long-term perspective. Understand that God's power is at work in you, even when the progress seems slow. Trust that each step, no matter how small, is moving you forward.

The dominion key is just a start. What is important is that you transfer the lessons you've learned about agency, growth, and patience into other parts of your life. It's a key to something, and that something is change.

Get after it. You have made a great start but that's all it is. The world is about to open before you.

Truth and Grace,
John

5

Building Relationships

SYNOPSIS: Christopher is a forty-five-year-old consultant who has always viewed relationships as a means to an end. As an introvert, he has few friends and most of his connections are work-based. When he changes jobs, he finds himself starting over, leading to a cycle of loneliness he would never openly admit. Christopher is also a believer, but he often operates as a lone ranger, avoiding deep connections and the vulnerability that comes with them. This chapter delves into Christopher's journey of understanding the importance of authentic relationships and how embracing vulnerability can lead to true companionship and a more fulfilling life.

SUBJECT:
Building Meaningful Relationships

Hi Christopher,

I hope this email finds you well. I've been reflecting on our recent conversations about friendship. Your current situation is common among American men: many have fewer friends than they would like. Some writers even refer to it as an epidemic of loneliness. That might be a bit strong in your case, but it's clear that you wish you had more friends.

Many men try to fill this gap by relying on their wives to take the place of missing guy friends. However, this approach doesn't work very well. While it's important to be great friends with your bride, relying on her as your only friend puts a lot of strain on the marriage.

Talking with you reminded me of a story from my own life, and I thought it might resonate with you. For much of my life, I experienced myself as an outsider. I described my experience of life as Ebenezer Scrooge from *A Christmas Carol*.[18] There is a place where Scrooge visits the Cratchit family and looks at them through the window. He sees their happy family celebrating Christmas while he stands in the cold. That perfectly describes how I felt in life—always on the outside, looking in.

At a retreat, I realized that the glass that separated me was of my own invention. I created the glass to keep me safe. It became the cage that kept me alone. I substituted respect for love. I knew how to get respect, but I had no idea how to get love. Love is only fully received in an undefended state, and I was never undefended. On that day, for the first time, I felt undefended, and it became the turning point of my life. I was finally open to receiving love, and it transformed me.

When I was in my early fifties, someone told me that relationships are the fuel of life. Everything that I've done since then has rippled out of that idea. When I turned fifty, I had a little birthday party with my friend group, three or four people, who came and made a funny hat for me. I lived a very small relational life. I was running a company, and most of my associates were people in the company. I had very few honest-to-goodness friends.

This began to change as I began to establish relationships. When I had my sixtieth birthday, my sweet wife and best friend threw a birthday party for me that had a hundred people at it. I remember walking into this restaurant down by the river here in Atlanta. It was almost like a wedding. It was a complete surprise to me. When I walked into that room, I knew the story of every man in the room and most of the women. That was the result of the changes in my fifties that left me living in a rich and supportive community.

You're not done changing until you decide you're done changing or you become senile. Building relationships was what gave me the ability to change. I always gave myself a pass for being an introvert, which I am. But as I changed, I developed the ability to see other people and make them feel seen. I became curious. I could sit down with somebody and say, tell me your story, and they would. As a result of that, I began to expand and develop relationships.

I know you're busy and feel you don't have time to build deep friendships, but you do. In fact, you can't afford not to. The time you invest in friendships is an investment that benefits your family and isn't just a cost. Building adult friendships is like dating: start with

> **Building adult friendships is like dating: start with breakfast or coffee.**

breakfast or coffee. If there's a connection, meet again. It's not magic; it takes time and may involve some false starts, but you will find your way.

Looking forward to hearing your thoughts.

Best,
John

SUBJECT:
Sarcasm

Hi Christopher,

I'm excited to hear you've decided to join our group. This journey of building deeper and more meaningful relationships can be incredibly rewarding. Before we dive in, I wanted to share a few thoughts with you about something I've noticed—sarcasm.

Sarcasm, especially among men, often becomes a default mode of communication. It's witty and can be funny, but it also creates separation and keeps people on the defensive. I've seen it time and again in various settings where sarcasm is the language of the realm. The humor was sharp, but it built walls instead of bridges.

When we're sarcastic or around sarcasm, we might share bits of our lives (being transparent), but we rarely share the deeper, more vulnerable parts. True connection requires vulnerability—offering up those parts of ourselves that we typically shield from the world. But no one feels safe to be vulnerable in a sarcastic environment. Sarcasm can quickly become a way to say harsh things without taking responsibility for the impact of our words. It's the language of cowards. We hit someone with a sarcastic joke, then dismiss their hurt by asking, "Can't you take a joke?" This deflection avoids accountability and undermines genuine communication, fostering a toxic environment where trust and openness are compromised.

> No one feels safe to be vulnerable in a sarcastic environment.

In our group, we aim to foster an environment of genuine support and understanding. This means creating a space where everyone feels safe to be themselves, without the fear of being mocked or belittled. I've seen firsthand how dropping sarcasm and embracing honesty can transform relationships.

When sarcasm is present, trust erodes. It keeps us from truly seeing and being seen. I encourage you to think about this as we move forward. Our goal is to build connections that go beyond the surface, where we can all feel safe to share our true selves.

I'm looking forward to the growth and deeper connections that will come from our time together. If you have any thoughts or questions before we get started, feel free to reach out.

Truth and Grace,
John

SUBJECT:
Embracing True Connection

Hi Christopher,

I am so glad you are part of our group. I'm also glad to hear that you feel like you told your real story to us—for the first time in your life. It's a significant step, and I'm honored you trusted us with it. When we put down our defenses and reveal our true selves, we almost always find acceptance. In fact, I don't think I've ever seen a case where someone experienced rejection when they told the truth about who they really are.

Remember, we're not here to fix you. We're here to love you. Relationships can't be taught through a course or a manual; they are experienced and witnessed. We don't care about your skills. You are precious to us as a person because you are a person, not because of your talent.

One concept that has been life-changing for me in our group is the idea of listening to learn. Most of us tend to listen to win, maneuvering conversations to where we want them to go. But listening to learn means being genuinely curious about what's going on inside the other person.

If I'm in a relationship and I'm listening to you in order to maneuver you toward what I think is the right answer, I don't really care about you. But, if I listen to learn, then I'm curious about what's happening inside you. I'm much more likely to ask a good question when I listen to you. Leading questions, like "Don't you see this is a failed strategy?" close off dialogue. Instead, asking, "You've been at this for a while and you're very persistent. Help me understand why you're so persistent in this course," opens up the conversation and fosters understanding.

When we listen to win, we're like lawyers, laying a line of questions down and then snapping the trap shut to make our point. That's not a real relationship. I'm not curious; I already know the answer and just need you to get to it. But real relationships are built on curiosity and genuine interest in each other.

Impressing people builds moats, not bridges. We often think that impressing others draws them toward us, but it actually creates distance. Sharing our successes might gain admiration, but it doesn't build connection. People connect to our grit, not to our shine. Confessing need attracts resources, while hiding need repels them. If you are perfect, then you don't need anything from me, and that doesn't build a relationship.

It may sound counterintuitive, but if you want to build a relationship with someone, ask them to do something for you rather than doing something for them. I had a bunch of flooring delivered to my house and, instead of hiring help, I called a few friends to help me move it into the basement. They jumped at the chance to help, and we grew closer because of it. When you ask for help, you are letting others into your life.

> **People connect to our grit, not to our shine.**

There's a powerful scene in the movie *Gladiator* where Russell Crowe's character is in a tunnel with a group of men.[19] He says, "I don't know what's waiting for us outside this tunnel. Whatever it is, we'll do better if we fight together rather than separately." When the doors open, they face chariots with archers. Some men went off alone and were quickly killed, but those who stayed with Crowe fought as a unit, repelling the attacks and eventually taking the offense. This scene is a great metaphor for us as Christians. Satan watches for those who go alone, as they are more easily overcome.

Do you want to be a man who fights bravely but dies quickly or do you want a band of brothers who give you a fighting chance?

Best,
John

SUBJECT:
Suffering

Hi Christopher,

I am so sorry to hear about your mother's passing. There is no one else in our lives that fills the same role that a mother does. Losing her must be incredibly painful, and my heart goes out to you during this difficult time.

You asked me about the point of pain and why Christians have to suffer. Shouldn't God just remove the pain and let us live pain-free lives? It would be nice if it worked that way, but it doesn't. In my experience, I've found that suffering produces empathy.

Some people are wired to accomplish things and are driven by their achievements. Often, these people don't have much mercy because their lives have been relatively bulletproof—they haven't faced many hardships. However, when you suffer—whether it's losing someone close to you, facing a serious illness, or losing your job—it fosters empathy for others. The Bible says that we comfort others with the comfort we have received (2 Corinthians 1:4, NIV). This comfort arises from our suffering, enabling us to extend it to others.

For instance, an executive who loses his job might create a job network for other executives in similar situations. His personal experience makes him more empathetic and less judgmental toward others facing the shame, fear and rejection of job loss. When we understand how difficult someone's struggles are, we're less likely to judge them.

Christianity is an individual decision and a team sport. It's meant to be lived in a community. We need people who function as protectors and encouragers for us. The Bible repeatedly uses the phrase "one another," emphasizing the importance of living closely with each other. We need each other, especially in our moments of weakness.

When my sister passed away in 2022, I encountered a range of responses to my grief. Some were genuinely helpful, while others missed the mark. Many people tried to offer insights or comforting wisdom in an effort to ease the pain. I found that the only truly comforting responses were simple expressions of love and presence, such as "I love you" and "I'm with you." During times of loss, it's the presence of others that brings the most comfort. Advice and insights often feel inadequate and sometimes offensive. What I needed most was for people to stand by me, attend the funeral, and offer sincere condolences like, "I'm here.

> **Christianity is an individual decision and a team sport.**

I know how much you loved your sister. I'm so sorry." Comments like "She's in a better place" or "God needed another angel" did not provide solace. In moments of deep grief, the presence and empathy of others are what truly comforts.

I'm not sure that we're born being empathetic toward others. Suffering produces empathy. When you meet someone who has never suffered and for whom everything has always come easily, they tend not to be very merciful. None of us get through life without suffering, and as we suffer, we become more empathetic toward others.

In the Christian community, we often aim to be encouragers, and rightly so. However, at the appropriate time and in the right manner, we should also be willing to discourage—clearly addressing what isn't working and even confronting issues when necessary. Our objective should be to act as healthy protectors, not mindless affirmers.

If you read the New Testament, you'll find that Jesus, at different times, moved toward people, moved away from them, and moved against them. These aren't moral categories; they are responses to what the person needs at that moment. Should you move toward them, create space, or oppose them? In every relationship, you will find yourself in one of these three spots.

Please know that I'm here for you, Christopher. If you need to talk, vent, or just have someone sit with you, I'm here.

With deepest sympathy,
John

SUBJECT:
Building Lasting Connections

Hi Christopher,

It has been so fun to see the immense change that has come over you by being part of our group. I know you have longed to find deeper relationships, and now you are doing such a great job of building those more intimate connections. But we can't always be best friends with everyone.

Anthropologist Robin Dunbar studied monkeys and later applied his findings to humans.[20] He wrote a book called *How Many Friends Does One Person Need?* He has coined an idea, now called Dunbar's Number, which explores the idea that we have concentric circles of intimacy in our lives. These circles include people who are very close to us, like our spouse, a group of about five people who are our most intimate friends, a group of about fifteen close friends, a group of fifty friends, and a group of one-hundred-and-fifty acquaintances.

I started to fill up my circles in my fifties. My circles had never been full–especially the close ones. I'm still an introvert and struggle with knowing a large number of people. There is a limit of about fifteen hundred people who we will recognize by name and know who they are. I focus more and more on putting my time and energy into fewer meaningful relationships.

One principle I've learned is that when we seek to impress people, we create distance instead of intimacy. When someone says, "You're so smart," or "You're so rich," it builds a moat between us. God has placed an innate desire in us to know others and to allow ourselves to be known by them. It can be scary to allow someone to know us deeply. But, when we do, and they don't run out of the room screaming, the world gets safer for us.

There is also a sense of relaxation that comes from spending time with friends. For our relationships to be fuel for us, we need to be relaxed. We don't need to be constantly defending ourselves. We don't need to be attacking or on guard. If I can be myself and experience the joy of being with you while you are being yourself, we can build a relationship. Neither one of us is hiding.

When there are walls between us, I'm constantly managing what everyone else thinks and what I'm going to say or not say. In our group, no one cares. We are just ourselves. That kind of group is life-giving. It is in this sense of relaxation that our greatest friendships grow.

Robertson McQuilkin, the former president of Columbia International University, exemplified this beautifully.[21] When his wife Muriel was diagnosed with Alzheimer's disease, he stepped away from his career to care for her. Many people disagreed with his decision, but he saw his commitment to his wife as the most important one. He famously said, "Those who don't build friendships in the spring and summer of life must find winter a lonely time." The best time to create a friend is thirty years ago. But the second best time is today. Unfortunately, you can never make an old friend.

Christopher, I'm so glad you're part of our group. I know that you and I have been forever changed by the opportunity to build these meaningful relationships together.

Regards,
John

6

Enjoying the Seasons of Life

SYNOPSIS: These emails serve as a follow-up to a recent meeting involving Mark, Jim, and Scott, each representing distinct stages of life—thirties, forties, and fifties. Through our discussions, it became apparent that each man is navigating unique seasons of life, each presenting its own set of challenges and impacting their respective situations differently.

SUBJECT:
The Joys and Challenges of Young Children

Dear Mark,

I hope this email finds you well. I wanted to reach out to you after our recent meeting and express my gratitude for your openness and honesty about the struggles you're facing as a father of three young children. Your candidness resonated with me, and I want you to know that you're not alone in feeling overwhelmed at times.

Raising children while juggling the demands of a corporate job is undoubtedly challenging. It's like navigating a bustling city where new challenges arise at every turn, and sometimes it feels like nothing new can be built without something else being torn down. The stress can be relentless. Parenting takes courage. You are going to invest countless hours in raising your kids, and you can't really be certain if you are "doing it right" or if it will all work out well. It's an act of faith.

As we discussed, childhood is a crucial phase where children learn both responsibility and independence, two traits that can sometimes conflict. This tension is natural, as many aspects of life involve balancing opposing forces. On one hand, successful children learn to be responsible. This can be seen in age-appropriate chores, taking care of themselves or a pet, planning their schoolwork, or getting ready on time. Responsible children do not need a parent constantly hovering over them, guiding each step and fighting every

> **Parenting takes courage.**

battle. Importantly, they have also learned to self-regulate their emotions and handle external demands.

However, being merely responsible is not enough to prepare children for adolescence. They also need to be independent. An independent child has established their own personality and has differentiated from their parents. They are curious and feel free to explore. An independent child does not always run to a parent for approval or direction. An independent child is courageous.

Do you see the tension? You are not raising an automaton, but you are not raising a feral child either. Yes, it's a tension, but the healthiest children I see are not just a little of one or the other. They are fully independent and fully responsible.

This might be a good moment to ride one of my hobby horses. While I use the word parenting, I try to keep fathering and mothering separate in my mind. You and your bride are not interchangeable parenting units. Each of you has a specific role to play in the development of your children that is not exactly the same as the other. I am reluctant to lay down dogmatic gender roles for everyone, but I recognize that your children need different things from each of you. If you don't find the strength to show up fully, something important will be missing.

It won't be hard to find people who bristle at the idea that fathers and mothers bring something different to the task of parenting, but it's been true for thousands of years. Nothing about the politics or conventions of the moment changes that. Your children need something different from you as their dad than they do from your wife. It might be easier for you to think this way than to be distracted by gender definitions. This takes thoughtfulness and creativity. Consider how to develop your child's independence and responsibility. While it's all weighty and demanding, it is also fun and brings great joy. It's a domain of life that calls forth your very best.

Your kids need to see you and your bride making your relationship important. Children are too often treated as the center of the universe when they should not be. They will draw comfort and security from the strength of your marriage and, unfortunately, will be hypersensitive to its frailties.

Modeling is more important than teaching. If you want to develop responsibility and independence in your children, you have to model it for them. Remember you are raising men and women, not boys and girls.

You are going to be a great dad, and I look forward to watching.

Warmly,
John

SUBJECT:
Your Thirties: A Voyage of Manhood

Dear Liam,

I hope this email finds you well amidst the whirlwind of life's demands. Thanks for sharing your recent update on the hectic pace and stresses of your life. It's important to recognize that what you are experiencing is a very normal part of what thirty-year-olds face. With that in mind, I wanted to take this opportunity to delve deeper into the unique challenges you're encountering in your thirties and offer some insights that may help you navigate this tumultuous period with more clarity and confidence.

Your description of the thirties as a decade filled with stress and uncertainty resonated deeply with my own experiences. I vividly recall this time of life, where the responsibilities of adulthood seemed to multiply exponentially, leaving me feeling as though I was constantly treading water in a sea of obligations. From balancing the demands of a challenging career to nurturing relationships with my spouse and children, the pressure often felt overwhelming. Looking down the road and thinking of future financial obligations such as college expenses, weddings, and retirement funding only added to the weight on my shoulders. Marriage had become more relationally challenging and I wondered what it would look like in the future. It was all like climbing a slippery pole, where every pull upward is accompanied by the fear of slipping back down the pole.

To make matters worse, the close friends you had in college might start melting away, leaving you with fewer confidants. The demands of life leave little time to nurture these relationships, leading us to believe we must navigate this journey alone. One day we wake up and find ourselves feeling lonely, wondering how we got to this point.

Take this the right way: you are not special. I wasn't either. As far as I can tell, this is the normal experience of thirty-year-old men in our culture. Actually, I hope you find a bit of comfort in realizing that your situation is common to your age and stage of life. If I had one thing to tell you, it would be: "You will get through this."

A transformative moment for me occurred while visiting the National Gallery of Art in Washington, DC, where I encountered a series of four paintings by Thomas Cole depicting a man's journey along the river of life.[22] Although painted in the 1840s, one of them profoundly impacted me. *The Voyage of Life: Manhood* really stood out. This powerful scene depicts a man navigating treacherous rapids and large boulders in a boat fashioned from angel wings, with an angel guiding the way at the helm. Although his situation looks hopeless, God is behind him watching from above; the man just can't see him. It is unclear whether there is a way through the river. With arms uplifted in prayer, he wrestles with the uncertainty of his fate.

Despite the depicted challenges, I found comfort in the realization that this turbulent phase is a natural part of life's journey. I bought a print of the painting, had it framed, and it still hangs over my desk. It serves as a flag that reminds me of our common journey. Similarly, your voyage through the stress of your thirties is marked by doubts, fears, and pressure. It's a decade defined by hard choices and difficult sacrifices. You're not alone in facing these challenges.

Your thirties are a bit of a storm. Many times you will need to have faith in the goodness of God and courage to keep going. Finding a band of brothers who are living similar lives and who face similar challenges can really help.

I often say that Christianity is both an individual decision and a team sport. Remember, you don't have to go it alone. A Puritan preacher once wrote, "Satan watcheth for he that sails without a convoy."[23] This is still true today. I'm grateful to be your mentor during this season of your life.

My thirties culminated in a profound encounter with God. It's challenging to describe, but amid the pressure of selling the company I had worked so hard to build, dealing with my parents' health issues, managing the demands of three children, and navigating a troubled marriage, my Heavenly Father spoke into my life. In many ways, the pressures and stresses of my thirties were the very path to true freedom.

Remember, Liam, that the challenges you're facing in your thirties are a natural part of life. You are doing the heavy lifting of carving out your life relationally, professionally, and personally. It is heavy lifting and there are times you won't be sure of the outcome. Embrace the uncertainty, lean into the discomfort, and trust that with perseverance and resilience, you will emerge stronger and wiser on the other side. Your Heavenly Father is so close.

Wishing you strength, courage, and clarity as you navigate the turbulent seas of your thirties.

Warm regards,
John

SUBJECT:
Reflecting on Our Discussion and Your Forties

Dear Jim,

I hope this email finds you well after our recent meeting. It was great to hear your perspective on life. Our conversation left me reflecting on the unique opportunities and challenges that come with navigating through the forties, and I wanted to share some thoughts with you.

Your forties represent a decade of choice and possibility. With years of hard work behind you, you have opportunities now to branch out and try something different. From our conversation, it's clear you have accumulated both financial and relational capital. This newfound stability grants you the freedom to make a new set of choices.

I loved your idea about starting your own consulting business. Your competence, energy, and innate talent make you the perfect person to begin helping others. As marriages settle and families grow more independent, the forties offer a chance to embark on new ventures. Whether it's starting a new business, changing careers, or simply making a lifestyle adjustment, you have the resources and resilience to take calculated risks. The beauty of this stage of life is that even if things don't go as planned, you have the time and ability to change direction and forge a new path forward. If everything turns out great, you have time to make the most of it.

Some people confuse this idea with a midlife crisis. I don't know if the notion of a midlife crisis is true or not. I certainly don't see it in everyone. The midlife crisis for some is a kind of romantic notion of abandoning your current life and its commitments in favor of adventure and pleasure. This implies rootlessness and a lack of grounding. There is also a subtle victimhood implicit in the idea that your circumstances and commitments are the problem. It's rarely true. The problem with running away is that you are still you.

The forties are often a time of introspection and reflection. Men who have worked hard to create opportunities in their life may find themselves disconnected from others and even from their own inner selves. One positive development for some men in their forties is the reestablishment of intimate friendships with other guys. John Eldridge describes this process using the concepts of the "Shallows," the "Middle," and the "Depths."[24]In the "Shallows," conversations are light and casual, often centering around sports. In the "Middle," men begin to discuss some of their personal challenges. In the "Depths," however, men talk about the longings of their heart and the disappointments of life. Men who can reestablish friendships in the "Depths" often find greater success in their forties.

With the choices that come in your forties, we also get the question, "Why?" Why am I working hard? What will success really look like for me? What is most important to me in this phase of life? This season of questioning is not a distraction. It's a needed re-examination of your life before the challenges of the coming decades. How you process these questions in your forties will set the stage for your fifties.

In my forties, I moved from a cold start-up to my own consulting business and to being CEO of a tech enabled service business. Possibilities seemed endless. I don't think I was unusual except for my willingness to change. I look back on these days with fondness as my confidence was high and options seemed plentiful. Toward the end of that decade, I began to reestablish long neglected relationships with other men. You might find this decade to be similar.

I hope you and Brenda have the opportunity to start traveling more too. These past few years, you have had your nose down, working hard, so this is a great time to put your head up and reconnect with your bride. You have possibilities in front of you. That is what makes it such a fun and exciting season. Exploring new destinations and experiences can enrich your lives and create lasting memories. It's a chance to rejuvenate and appreciate the beauty of the world around you while also strengthening your bond as a couple.[24] Embrace this opportunity to step outside your comfort zone and discover new adventures together.

Our discussion also reminded me of the importance of reassessment and reaffirmation in this stage of life. Rather than discarding past decisions, most people in their forties find themselves doubling down on their commitments and embracing their chosen path with renewed vigor.

People think of their lives in their forties through one of several lenses. One of those lenses is a victim, you are the prisoner of your circumstances and of the choices of others. People who use this lens are reliably unhappy and are usually low performing. Another is the lens of agency. While you cannot do anything (that would make you sovereign, (which you are not), you do have a significant degree of freedom which is yours to exercise. Happy and successful people claim their agency and choose happiness. It's part of what makes being forty a wonderful time of life.

Claiming your agency requires courage. Floating along requires little from you. Making a choice and acting on it carries the risks of error or failure. Neither one will kill you. Try to make good decisions, but don't be afraid. What seems like a mistake when you are forty-two might look like the best choice ever ten years later.

Wishing you continued success and fulfillment on your journey. As we navigate our forties, it's natural to ponder life's purpose. However, this existential questioning isn't exclusive to midlife. We all have a priority, one value that brings order to all of our roles and responsibilities. What is that priority for you? For me, my relationship with God is my priority. I live not just for the present, but with an eye toward the next life. This perspective shapes how I approach each day.

Martin Luther taught that the purpose of all of our vocations is to love our neighbor.[25] He would have understood vocation as our various callings—husband, father, friend, and business person. "Who is my neighbor?" is the Pharisee's question. The answer is the person right in front of you. My neighbor in my calling as a husband is my wife. My neighbor as a business person is my employees, my customers, and my suppliers. It's really quite simple, but it's not easy.

John

SUBJECT:
The Challenges of Raising an Adolescent

Dear Jim,

I hope this message finds you and Brenda well. Thank you for sharing your recent struggles with me. Parenting through adolescence is undoubtedly one of the most challenging journeys we undertake, and your concerns about Hunter and Kristen resonate with me deeply.

If the business of childhood is developing responsibility and independence, adolescence revolves around developing identity. Teenagers are easily influenced. Their surrounding culture is bombarding them with ideas and messages that are not in their best interest. Navigating questions of identity can be particularly daunting. Teenagers often "try on" identities and then try out another the next week. That is why it is crucial that they don't make long-term decisions about identity. Their brains are immature and have not fully developed. However, the primary task of being an adolescent is figuring out this business of identity. Identity is the story you tell yourself about yourself.

Adolescence can be cruel and our kids can be exposed to really harsh and unkind stories about themselves that then become a big part of their identity. You are a bulwark against the condemning voices of their peers.

One way to think of dealing with your adolescent is "King Kong Parenting." Hang with me here for a moment. When children are small we have to strap them down to keep them from hurting themselves and others. But eventually, they leave for college or work and all your constraints will be gone. Your job as a parent is to gradually remove those straps and constraints. If you remove them too fast, your child will make potentially damaging choices. If you remove them too slowly, you will greatly hinder their development and make it much less likely that they will be successful on their own.

In our house, we had the idea that all restraints should be gone before their senior year in high school. That meant, to the greatest degree possible, they would live their last year at home without house rules. They experienced freedom while they were still at home. It also gave us some urgency about removing constraints all along. Your goal is not to raise children but to raise adults. The long view matters.

There will come a time when your child steps fully out of your control and provision. It's important for kids to see that moment coming long in advance of its arrival. One day, soon enough, they will be adults and will make their own choices but will carry the responsibility of those decisions too.

I am not particularly a fan of self-esteem. I think the self-esteem movement was founded on weak science. Fostering self-esteem in children and adolescents by affirmations ungrounded in reality has largely been a failure. On the other hand, I am a big fan of self-respect since it comes out of achievement and accomplishment. Self-respect is the result of hard, focused work.

I've come to understand that while parents can certainly influence their children's decisions, they cannot dictate them. You can guide and support your children, but ultimately, they will discover their own answers. A wise parent will establish a close connection with their child to maintain influence. However, if you're preoccupied with enforcing rules and consequences, your ability to influence may be limited. Rules by their nature promote rebellion. My sister used to say that she never thought about putting a bean up her nose until someone told her not to do it. Building a strong relationship is key to fostering influence with your child, rather than solely focusing on behavioral management. Who you are, not what you say, is their most important guardrail.

I've often relied on what I term my "magic triangle." This concept suggests that as parents of teenagers, we should spend about seventy percent of our time engaging in companionship with our child, twenty percent in teaching, and ten percent in correction. When faced with a situation where correction becomes more prominent, such as when a child gets in trouble, it becomes imperative to increase the time spent in companionship accordingly. This adjustment ensures that we maintain a strong connection with our child, even during challenging times. It's often a very difficult lesson. But, I've found that little triangle to be magic in fostering a healthy parent-child relationship.

As Christians we are understandably concerned about our children's spiritual development. It's something we cannot control but can influence. My most important goal was that I would raise godward kids, not popular or successful kids. My goal was important because it kept me from sending a mixed message to my children about what was important to me. My wife and I could be open about our own faith and how we made decisions, but we couldn't control theirs.

Kids listen to you until they are about fifteen. Then they stop. Your mouth moves and noise comes out, but they are not hearing you. Instead, they are watching you...like a hawk. They want to know if you really believe what you say you believe. They are not demanding perfection, only congruence. If your life, as they observe it, lines up with what you say is most important to you, they will give it a shot. However, if it doesn't, the adolescent will decide they are on their own since Mom and Dad don't really believe what they say they do.

We should think about parenting the heart, not enforcing our rules. When there is a heart issue, we might need to intervene as lightly as possible, always with a view to the adolescent's heart. In the end, behavior matters much less than their heart condition.

Adolescence is indeed a tumultuous time, marked by rapid changes and intense emotions. Psychoanalyst Erik Erikson's insights into identity formation during this stage are particularly relevant, highlighting the critical role that parents play in shaping their children's sense of self.[26]

While adolescents may appear to push us away, they are still deeply influenced by our words, actions, and our character.

Remember, parenting is a journey filled with ups and downs, but your love and dedication to your children will see you through even the toughest challenges. Adolescence requires considerable courage from a teenager, and it necessitates an infinite wellspring of courage from parents.

Wishing you and Brenda strength and patience as you continue to navigate the joys and trials of parenthood.

Warm regards,
John

SUBJECT:
Embracing Authority In Your Fifties

Dear Scott,

I hope this letter finds you in good spirits as you navigate the peak of your journey through the decade of the fifties. This is a time of remarkable significance, where the culmination of your years of hard work and dedication converge into a season of authority and influence.

Your fifties mark the pinnacle of your professional prowess. With decades of experience under your belt, you possess a wealth of knowledge and expertise. You have health and energy. Your brain, still young and supple enough to adapt, serves as a formidable tool in tackling the challenges that come your way. While you are not likely to solve novel problems in new ways, you certainly know how to work the knobs and dials at your job. The fifties can be a really good decade.

One of the unique aspects of being in your fifties is the ability to relate to individuals across generations. You're young enough to connect with those in their twenties, sharing insights and guidance gleaned from your own journey. Simultaneously, you command a level of respect and gravitas from those in their sixties and seventies, earning authority that is legitimate.

Yet, with authority comes responsibility. It's a burden that you carry not for personal gain, but for the benefit of others. Authority, when wielded wisely and with humility, can bring about positive change and transformation. However, it's essential to recognize that authority is not meant to be held indefinitely. Like a torch passed from one hand to another, there will come a time when you must lay down this mantle of power, allowing others to step into leadership roles and carry the torch forward.

Lord Acton's famous adage, "Power tends to corrupt, and absolute power corrupts absolutely," serves as a poignant reminder of the dangers of clinging to authority for too long.[27] As you approach the latter years of your fifties, it's natural to contemplate what lies ahead and try to hold onto power at all costs. I liked the authority that came from being a CEO. I wielded it well, but there came a time when I laid it down. Now there is not one person on earth who has to do what I tell them to do!

In essence, authority is not the ultimate prize; it's a temporary burden entrusted to us for the betterment of others. Influence waits on the other side of authority. In many ways, it's a much more powerful tool. As we transition from wielding authority to exerting influence, may we do so with grace, wisdom, and a deep sense of purpose. Start thinking.

John

SUBJECT:
Celebrating the Transformative Twenties

Dear Scott,

Thanks for following up on my last email and sharing the concerns and frustrations that you and Cindy have about Ryan. I can sense the weight of your worries about his choices and future path, especially with his decision to pursue music and drop out of college. It's understandable that you're seeking clarity and direction in navigating this phase of his life.

I'm a bit of an outlier when I express my fondness for the twenties. Most Boomers like me were horrified by the Millennials and offended by the Zoomers. Not me. There's unparalleled magic and potential during this phase of life that I find incredibly captivating. While I understand your desire for Ryan to grow up, it's crucial to recognize and feed this unique phase instead of squelching it. Throughout history, countless visionaries and innovators, from Albert Einstein to Picasso, have left an indelible mark on the world during their twenties. Picasso's work in his twenties changed art. His work in his sixties still showed his undeniable talent but it was no longer revolutionary. Einstein won the Nobel Prize for work he did in his twenties. Think of tech giants like Microsoft and Apple, both founded by individuals in their twenties, or legendary musicians such as The Beatles, Elvis, and Taylor Swift, who made their most significant contributions during this transformative decade. It's a time characterized by exploration, experimentation, and the pursuit of lofty dreams.

It's also essential to recognize the significance of the twenties as a transformative decade. Our twenties are traditionally the decade during which we finish our formal education and decide whom to marry, where to live, and what kind of work we will do. I've also found that the more intense the environment, the more intense the relationship. In the crucible of the twenties, where every decision carries weight, relationships take on heightened significance. Some of the most intense relationships are formed in the heat of battle with shared experiences and struggles fostering unique and enduring connections.

Another aspect to consider is the remarkable capacity and exuberance of individuals in their twenties. The frontal cortex of the brain, responsible for decision-making and judgment, is still developing during this time. This lack of fully matured judgment allows for creativity, fearlessness, and willingness to take risks. It's a time when individuals are exploring their passions and testing their boundaries, often with boldness and determination. Twenty-year-olds don't have any better sense than to try something magnificent. While we might hesitate or feel too tired to even try, your son keeps going into the early hours of the morning. His boundless energy and audacity should be celebrated and encouraged.

While it's natural to feel concerned about Ryan's unconventional path, it's his path. You had eighteen years to form him, and now it's not your job. Unsolicited advice is always perceived as criticism. Whether you know it or not, your words weigh 800 pounds. They carry a weight, for good or ill, that is out of proportion because you said them. I would suggest that you be a cheerleader for your son until he asks you for your opinion. It's important to acknowledge the value of his pursuits and the potential for growth and discovery. Adolescents don't mature until they experience the benefits and consequences of their choices. We might be reluctant to allow that, but by doing so, we are only hindering their development.

I understand your concerns about Ryan's future and the desire for him to embrace responsibility. It's essential to have open and honest conversations with him about his goals, aspirations, and the steps he plans to take to achieve them. By fostering a supportive and understanding environment, you can guide him through this transformative phase, empowering him to face life's challenges with resilience and determination.

In the coming years, Ryan will continue to evolve and mature, discovering his strengths, values, and purpose. As parents, your role is to provide guidance, encouragement, and unwavering support as he embarks on this journey of self-discovery and personal growth.

I'm here to offer support as you help Ryan navigate this phase of his life. Together, we can help him embrace his potential and chart a course that aligns with his passions and aspirations.

Warm regards,
John

SUBJECT:
The Influence of the Sixties

Dear Scott,

I'm glad to hear that you are feeling more at peace with Ryan's choices. Moving your relationship from that of a parent who controls the situation to coming alongside him as a mentor and guide takes time. However, it is worth the effort. Keep the course, and you will be amazed to discover how your relationship might unfold.

Now that you have reached your sixties, you will often find the familiar landscape of authority shifting toward the influence that comes with experience and wisdom. While this prospect can evoke a mix of uncertainty and reflection, you will be able to accomplish much more with influence than you ever could with authority. Smart people learn to wield influence.

Authority is legitimized power. Influence is the ability to affect the beliefs and actions of others without power.

I remember an encounter with Andrew Young, the former mayor of Atlanta and ambassador of the United Nations. Although he no longer held these positions and had no real authority, his influence was enormous. I was the stranger in a room filled with admiration and reverence. I witnessed firsthand the power of influence that transcends mere organizational authority. The impact of Ambassador Young's words and actions was palpable, moving mountains with little more than a phone call and a heartfelt request. I've never seen anything quite like it, highlighting influence over authority.

The sixties usher in a decade where the currency of influence holds greater sway than the blunt force of authority. While authority may have provided avenues for accomplishment in our fifties, it's in our sixties that we discover the true potency of influence, stemming not from titles or positions, but from the depth of character and the authenticity of our connections.

It's a season where we trade the exhaustion of wielding authority for the invigorating role of mentorship and guidance. Stepping into this new phase, you will have the opportunity to leverage your wealth of experience and vast networks to effect meaningful change and inspire the next generation.

In your sixties, the world becomes your classroom, and your interactions with younger minds take on a profound significance. Through intentional mentorship and genuine connection, you will have the privilege of speaking into the lives of those who will shape the future, imparting wisdom, and fostering growth in ways that transcend the limitations of formal authority. Embrace the transformative power of influence, recognizing that your greatest legacy lies not in the positions held, but in the lives touched. Your impact will be felt by those who follow you.

John

SUBJECT:
The 70s, 80s, and Beyond

Hi Scott,

I hope this email finds you and Cindy well. Your questions about what to expect in your 70s, 80s, and beyond have prompted me to reflect on my own journey and the wisdom shared by those who have walked this path before me.

As someone who is now in my seventies, I've had the opportunity to witness the ebb and flow of life's seasons firsthand. Each decade brings its own unique challenges and joys, shaping us in ways we might never have imagined.

Entering one's seventies is indeed a time of reflection. I believe that your seventies are a decade of loss. It is a time of attending more funerals than ever before. You are more likely to experience health challenges in your seventies than in any prior decade. However, research tells us that our seventies are also a decade of contentment. As you navigate the challenges of aging, the ability to face loss with grace and courage becomes increasingly important. It is also very likely that you and Cindy will not age evenly, so that adds another layer of complexity to the journey.

I've often found myself pondering what lies ahead in my 80s and 90s, although I haven't personally experienced this stage of life. However, through countless conversations with individuals who have ventured into their eighth decade and beyond, I've gained valuable insights into what to expect. The fear of falling, both physically and mentally, becomes more pronounced. This decade often brings a heightened sense of self-awareness as health concerns take center stage. People tend to become more candid and straightforward in their interactions, with a decreased tolerance for trivialities. While their blunt honesty may sometimes be challenging, it is often appreciated for its authenticity and truthfulness.

As you age, your world can either get larger or smaller with the newfound freedom at your disposal. Some people become more self-centered while others choose to enrich their lives by including people in their life. However, as you approach eighty, it's common for our horizons to shrink due to diminishing energy and cognitive flexibility. But, I've learned that you're only done changing when you decide that you're done changing. As long as you have your wits about you, you have the ability to change long into life.

Scott, I want to reassure you that while the road ahead will have its obstacles, there is also immense beauty and fulfillment to be found in each stage of life. Courage is required for the adventure. As you and Cindy prepare to embark on this journey, know that you are not alone. There are people who care about you and are here to offer guidance and assistance whenever you need it.

John

7

Navigating Risk and Fear

SYNOPSIS: A conversation with James, a fifty-two-year-old business owner who has been successful, but as his business has grown, he has become more averse to risk, both personally and professionally. He does not want to have a big failure for which he could be criticized. He has become uncomfortable with the ambiguity of leadership. He often complains of burnout.

SUBJECT:
Burnout

Dear James,

I received your message about feeling burned out, and I wanted to share some thoughts with you. It's not uncommon for successful individuals like yourself to experience a sense of malaise or weariness as they navigate the challenges of running a business. They are quick to label this as a feeling of burnout, but I am not so sure. I have only worked with two men who I believed were burned out. In both cases they worked at the limit of their capacity for months. Eventually their body and mind simply said "enough," and they had to stop. Their burnout was real, but in my experience, rare.

When someone mentions feeling burned out, I often find that it's more a result of having lost focus rather than genuine exhaustion. You've always struck me as someone who takes great care of himself, maintaining a healthy lifestyle and exercising control over your schedule. At fifty-two-years old and in good health, you have the capacity to handle more than you might think.

Instead, I think you're bored. I think you've mistaken the rim of the rut for the horizon. Sometimes, what's needed is not more rest or vacation time, but rather a new challenge or responsibility that reignites your passion and enthusiasm. I recall a friend of mine who found himself in a similar situation. He seemed to be burned out, deeply tired, and feeling a bit hopeless. Some might have said he needed a break to rest, but the opposite was true.

My friend ended up adding a big new responsibility into his life. Although he almost doubled his workload, he came back alive because he wasn't bored anymore. His added responsibilities required a whole new level of effort, but they also unleashed a fresh wave of energy too. Again, doubling down, rest, recuperation, or more vacation time won't solve the problem. The solution is to run some risk, do something new.

We use the word "passion" to describe a feeling of excitement or enthusiasm. One client likened it to the feeling he got when the University of Georgia football team ran onto the field. In this scenario, he was just a spectator looking for a rush of exuberance. However, true passion is not about excitement or enthusiasm. Properly understood, the word "passion" connects to suffering. We are passionate about the things for which we are willing to suffer. In the football analogy, the genuine passion does not come from the spectators in the stands, but from the young men who endured Kirby Smart's rigorous summer practices in the hot Georgia sun. They suffered because they cared deeply about achieving their goals.

I encourage you to consider what new challenges or endeavors you could pursue to engage your passion and sense of purpose. Remember, the antidote to exhaustion is not necessarily rest, but rather whole-hearted engagement.

I look forward to hearing your thoughts on this matter.

Warm regards,
John

SUBJECT:
Navigating Fear and Risk

Dear James,

I appreciate you sharing thoughts with me about your struggle with fear and risk. It's clear that you're facing some significant challenges in navigating the uncertainties of leadership, and I want to offer some insights that might help you find a path forward.

First, it's important to recognize that leadership inherently involves ambiguity and uncertainty. No leader can predict with absolute certainty what will work and what won't. Some people thrive in this environment, embracing the unknown as an opportunity for growth and innovation.

However, it's apparent that you've become uncomfortable with this level of risk and uncertainty, fearing both the outcome and the process itself.

> **Leadership inherently involves ambiguity and uncertainty.**

Your tendency to view life in terms of perfect success or perfect failure is a common trait. This fear of failure and criticism may have been instilled in you early in life, driving you to strive for perfection and avoid criticism. However, this mindset can lead to procrastination and avoidance, particularly during critical moments when decisive leadership is needed. One famous historian described successful leaders as those who "accept at the striking hour, or the dangerous post, the responsibility for full and effective action."[28] I love that. As a leader you have to be ready in the moment it's required to act fully and effectively. There really is no time or room for dithering about the possibility for failure or criticism.

One important lesson you will learn as a leader is that you will never be perfect. It simply isn't possible. If "perfect" and "failure" are your only options, it will take a terrible toll on you to always see your failures. You have to see a third door that's always been there. It's called "good enough." You are going to go through that door more times than you will go through the "perfect" door. Take a moment and ask yourself: When have I ever done something perfectly? If you are honest with yourself, you'll likely conclude that such instances are rare, if not nonexistent. Your mind can always find something that could have been done better or quicker. Regardless of your efforts, you are critical of yourself.

Instead of fixating on unattainable perfection, I encourage you to celebrate your achievements and take a victory lap. Acknowledge your accomplishments when something goes well. Take a moment to revel in the successes, not because they were flawless, but because they were satisfactory—that, in itself, is a triumph.

At lower levels of your organization, your fear of making mistakes may have appeared as high achievement because you were working so hard to avoid mistakes. But, as the CEO of your company, you have to transcend mere rule following, or it will hinder your ability to take bold, decisive action. Being caught in a cycle of fear can severely limit your capacity to lead effectively. Pursuing opportunity will always lead to higher returns than fixing problems.

Changing deeply ingrained personality traits can be challenging, but it's not impossible. One key realization for you is that perfection is an unattainable goal. No matter how hard you try, there will always be imperfections and areas for improvement. Learning to embrace the concept of "good enough" can be liberating, allowing you to celebrate successes without fixating on perceived failures. Finding the "perfect door" is a myth.

How can you stop criticizing yourself so much? One way is to surround yourself with supportive and accepting friends who can help quiet your inner critic. Amplify relationships that foster trust and acceptance, and distance yourself from those who are overly critical or negative. By cultivating a more positive and accepting environment, you can gradually silence the voice of self-doubt and criticism within.

Furthermore, recognize that your criticism of others carries a special danger. The Bible says that we will be judged by the measure we use to judge others. By refraining from harsh judgment and cultivating a more accepting attitude toward others, you can reduce your tendency to be overly critical of yourself. Criticism is like a boomerang, often coming back with equal force. By fostering a mindset of acceptance and support for others, you can create a more positive internal dialogue and approach to leadership.

As a CEO, it is essential for you to draw reasoned and necessary conclusions that some may perceive as judgments—this is an essential part of your job. However, what is not part of your job is to engage in daily, unneeded conclusions about others that feed your own tendency toward self-criticism.

The Apostle Paul explains that judgment will occur at the end, when all our motives and actions will be fully revealed (1 Corinthians 4:5, NIV). Until then, we should minimize our judgments. Marcus Aurelius, the Stoic philosopher, said, "You always own the option of having no opinion. There is never any need to get worked up or to trouble your soul about things you can't control. These things are not asking to be judged by you. Leave them alone."[29] Having no opinion about many things might give you a lot of freedom.

In other words, embracing the middle ground between perfection and failure, surrounding yourself with supportive relationships, and fostering a culture of acceptance can help you overcome your fear of risk and criticism. It's a journey that may take time and effort, but you can quiet your inner critic and lean into decisions with confidence.

I look forward to hearing your thoughts and continuing our discussion on this important topic.

Warm regards,
John

SUBJECT:
Summoning Courage

Dear James,

It's understandable to feel overwhelmed when facing significant decisions or changes. Procrastination almost always is driven by fear, particularly the fear of not meeting expectations or facing criticism. Perfectionists, like yourself, may find this struggle amplified because of an aversion to making mistakes and being criticized. You may fear not doing something right so much that you don't do anything.

While being nice is often admired in the church world, there are moments when we must summon the required courage to stand firm in our convictions and take decisive action. Courage is the force that propels wisdom and justice into action, ensuring that they aren't just ideals but tangible realities.

Consider the scenario unfolding at a board meeting tonight. The owner of a company is fighting with the company's new president

> **Courage is the force that propels wisdom and justice into action**

who is trying to take over the company. The owner, a genuinely nice person, is going to have to fight for her own company and take it back from the grasp of the man trying to hijack what is not his. She might be afraid, but her role as the owner and guardian of the values means that she will have to act strongly to safeguard her company.

Merely being a nice person isn't going to get it done. She's going to have to be a good person who has the courage to confront a difficult situation head-on and take clear control of her company. She is going to have to tell this man he is either going to come into alignment with her leadership, or today will be his last day. And, if he doesn't come perfectly into alignment, take him by his belt loops and his collar and march him out the front door. I think she'll be able to do it.

Does that distinction between being nice and good seem strange to you? It does to some people. Nice is a word that conveys being pleasant and inoffensive. Good, on the other hand, is a virtue rooted in what is true and right. John Lewis, the famous civil rights leader and congressman, had this idea of "good trouble."[30] Sometimes we need to make trouble to fight for what is right, true, and good. In the end, mere niceness is weak. Courage is the executor of goodness, and goodness is strong.

Fear often clouds our judgment and inhibits our ability to act with conviction. However, what's remarkable is that courage, even in small doses, can overcome these barriers. All it takes is a few brief moments—a mere ten seconds—to initiate the conversation or action that sets everything else in motion. Can you find ten seconds of courage?

> **Can you find ten seconds of courage?**

Remember, courage isn't the absence of fear but the willingness to act in spite of it. Find those few seconds of courage, take the first step, and trust that the rest will follow. Lay aside being a nice guy and focus instead on being a good one.

Take heart, my friend, and know that I'm here to support you every step of the way.

Warm regards,
John

SUBJECT:
Building Relationships

James,

Your inquiry into the significance of friendships is a profound one, touching on the essence of human connection and its impact on our lives. Allow me to share some insights that may shed light on why cultivating close personal relationships is indeed crucial.

I have found that things that are broken in a relationship find healing in a relationship. Often, the fear of failure and aversion to risk that we experience stem from relational dynamics established early in life. They can be healed only within the context of trusting relationships, where we can find the courage to confront fears and navigate through adversity with greater resilience.

When surrounded by friends who genuinely care for our well-being, the perceived risks of life diminish, and we feel emboldened to face challenges head-on. The amount of discipline required from you will increase or decrease depending on the quality of your friends.

Henri Nouwen wrote, "There is within you a lamb and a lion. Spiritual maturity is the ability to let the lamb and lion lie down together. Your lion is your adult, aggressive self. It is your initiative-taking and decision-making self. But there is also your fearful, vulnerable lamb, the part of you that needs affection, support, affirmation, and nurturing."[31] Nouwen did a good job capturing the tension of a leader to act and take the initiative while accepting the affirmation and nurture they need. He is drawing a picture of an integrated life. The lion of drive and accomplishment is comfortable lying down with the lamb of relational need. In my journal, I have noted twenty-one relational needs of a leader. We all have these needs; why pretend otherwise?

The significance of friendships extends beyond personal comfort to the business world. Close personal bonds, fostered through trust and acceptance, can significantly impact one's courage and decision-making in business. The support and encouragement received from friends and family bolster our confidence and fortitude, enabling us to take risks and pursue opportunities with greater conviction.

A seminal Harvard study, known as the Vaillant Study, conducted over eighty-five years, underscored the profound influence of relationships on human well-being.[32] The study followed undergraduate students from Harvard University throughout their lives to identify the predictors of healthy aging. The core conclusion was that "the warmth of relationships throughout life has the greatest positive impact on life satisfaction," transcending the challenges of a difficult upbringing or adverse circumstances. Interestingly, the warmth of relationships was more positively correlated with business success and income than intelligence.

Relationships are the fuel of life. I heard this sentence from author Henry Cloud at his Ultimate Leadership seminar, and it has shaped the last two decades of my life.[33] Relationships are not the purpose of life; our purpose lies in serving others. However, relationships provide the fuel—they keep us moving ahead, offering energy and encouragement.

We might have a lot of relationships but relatively few intimate friends. Robin Dunbar proposed a structure of friendships in concentric circles of decreasing intimacy.[34] It's a helpful construct. We are only able to sustain a small number of intimate friends because of the time and energy required. Intimate and close friendships are characterized by high levels of vulnerability and trust. We have an inherent desire to know and be known. This is part of why the current loneliness epidemic in Western societies is so tragic.

Many people confuse camaraderie with friendship. A buddy is not necessarily the same thing as a friend. Friendship has three requirements. First, there has to be some level of admiration. If there is nothing admirable about this other person, you won't be able to form a deep attachment to them. No one is perfect or perfectly admirable. We all have our faults, even big ones, but friends find something to admire in their friends. The second requirement is common values. No one will match perfectly, but friends have values that are in many ways congruent. The final requirement is chemistry. It's magic and hard to describe, but it is essential for friendship to exist. Without chemistry, a deeper friendship is unlikely to form.

The Dunbar concept of concentric circles of relationship has been very helpful to me. According to this concept, there are varying levels of closeness among our relationships, ranging from intimate friends to casual acquaintances. Recognizing this helps me understand that not everyone needs to be a close friend, but this does not mean they need to be cut off. Instead, they only belong to one of the other circles. There is no point in creating enmity where it does not exist.

I have an idea that might be a bit controversial, and while I can't prove it definitively, I believe it's true: most of our emotional needs are met by same-gender relationships. We often place too much pressure on marriage to meet all of our needs, neglecting other relationships. To have healthy marriages, we also need strong friendships.

Consider for a moment the concept of moats and magnets. Some behaviors in relationships act like moats, creating emotional distance from others and serving as self-protective mechanisms. Other behaviors function as magnets, attracting people to us.

Trouble arises when we get the two things confused. Some people think impressing others is a magnet, but it acts more like a moat. Sarcasm, too, is mistakenly seen as a magnet when it's almost always a moat—and a destructive one at that. Sarcasm is the language of cowards, not friends. On the other hand, expressing need is often seen as a moat, yet it functions as a magnet, drawing people closer.

Getting your moats and magnets right is vital for creating and sustaining productive relationships. Building friendship is a risky business and requires exposing yourself to the possibility of rejection. Rejection is unpleasant but not fatal. The reward of genuine connection far outweighs the risk. Summon your courage and move into it.

Wishing you clarity and strength as you navigate the intricate tapestry of human connection.

Rejection is unpleasant but not fatal.

Warm regards,
John

Dear James,

In our journey through leadership, one of the most profound realizations we encounter is the stark difference between following and leading—a contrast epitomized by the metaphor of driving through the fog.

Imagine yourself at night on the winding Pacific Coast Highway, between the cliff and a mountain, shrouded in thick fog. Only the dim glow of your headlights pierces through the mist. Looking ahead, you follow the two red dots of the taillights in front of you. You can't see anything else. The traffic following behind you does the same thing.

For most of our careers, we're content to follow the taillights of those ahead, relying on their guidance and precedent to navigate the uncertain terrain. But then, with a promotion or a significant shift in responsibility, you find yourself at the front, staring into the opaque expanse ahead—the "white" of the fog.

Suddenly, there are no more reassuring taillights to follow, no pre-defined path to tread. Instead, you're confronted with the unsettling reality of uncertainty and risk. This is the essence of leadership—the willingness to venture into the unknown, to embrace ambiguity, and to confront the possibility of failure head-on.

Navigating the fog of uncertainty can be disorienting. When you're enveloped in the whiteness of the fog, the edges of the road blur, and the hidden precipice of the cliff lurks ominously in your mind. The fear is palpable—you're acutely aware that a misstep could send everyone hurtling over the edge. As you grapple with the weight of leadership, you find yourself asking, "What am I going to tell all these people to do?"

I recall a man who, on his first day as a leader, wrestled with imposter syndrome. Entering the office, he grappled with feelings of inadequacy, doubting his ability to guide his team. In reality, he was one of the smartest executives I have ever known. He even took an IQ test to join Mensa, the society for geniuses, as a means to meet Michael Porter, a renowned professor of strategy at Harvard Business School. But that morning, he was gripped by fear of inadequacy. What he didn't realize was that this feeling of inadequacy is universal—nobody truly has all the answers, and everyone is, to some extent, just making it up as they go along.

A friend of mine, who oversees a national organization with several billion dollars in revenue, candidly admitted, "Sixty percent of the time, I really don't know what I'm doing. I just make the best decision I can." A little imposter syndrome is not necessarily bad; it keeps you on your toes. However, when it starts to dominate your thinking, it becomes paralyzing.

Winston Churchill gave a truly generous eulogy to Neville Chamberlain, the man he replaced as prime minister. Churchill said, "The only guide to a man is his conscience; the only shield to his memory is the rectitude and sincerity of his actions. It is very imprudent to walk through life without this shield, because we are so often mocked by the failure of our hopes and the upsetting of our calculations; but with this shield, however the fates may play, we march always in the ranks of honor."[35]

Rectitude, a seldom used word, means morally correct behavior or thinking. It came from a French word meaning "straight."

What he meant is that throughout history, whether we succeeded or failed may be interpreted differently. But the mark of true leadership lies not in the certainty of outcomes but in the steadfast adherence to one's values and conscience, even in the face of uncertainty. It's about taking action guided by conviction, even when the path ahead is shrouded in fog.

Leadership is synonymous with risk. It's taking action in an environment of uncertainty where you don't know if it will work. You use your best judgment and hope it does, but if you are certain then it's not a risk. What separates the leaders from the managers is that leaders know it might not work, but they do it anyway. They take the risk.

Leaders recognize that success often hinges on their willingness to venture beyond the safety of the familiar—to chart new courses, seize new opportunities, and confront new challenges. As the Chinese proverb aptly puts it, "When winds of change blow, the foolish man builds a wall, and the wise man builds a windmill."[36]

History is replete with examples of organizations that thrived on the cusp of uncertainty, seizing opportunities. Conversely, those that recoiled from risk and clung to the safety of the status quo invariably found themselves mired in decline. Organizations that fail to take risks commensurate with their size will enter their decline. Standing pat is not a long-term option. Neither is playing small ball. Risk is required for economic and organizational vitality.

> Leadership is synonymous with risk.

Take, for instance, the cautionary tale of Coca-Cola—a once-mighty company that now languishes in the twilight of its former glory. Faced with the imperative to dare greatly, Coca-Cola faltered, eschewing the risks necessary for continued relevance. Coke has not taken a meaningful risk in a generation. History is filled with examples of companies who ceased to take risks and then declined. If we stop pursuing new opportunities and shy away from risks, we risk facing a similar fate.

But amidst the fog of uncertainty lies boundless potential—the opportunity to harness change, seize advantage, and redefine the future. So, my friend, as you confront the white expanse of uncertainty before you, remember that leadership is not about avoiding risk but about embracing it. It's about being the one to build the windmill when others opt for the safety of walls.

Choose risk, but choose it wisely.

With warm regards,
John

SUBJECT:
Finding Courage

Dear James,

Fear, when appropriately channeled, leads to action—it prompts us to respond swiftly to potentially dangerous situations, much like moving away from a venomous snake in your garage. However, anxiety is different; it's like an addictive attachment to fear, immobilizing us without productive action. It is as if I worry about the snake but then don't move away. I leave myself open to getting bitten. Even worse is when your anxiety is over something that hasn't happened or is only remotely possible. In that case, anxiety has formed an addictive relationship with fear.

The remedy lies in active engagement—whenever fear grips you, take a step forward. Even a small action can begin to dissolve fear, gradually building courage and making the anxiety dissipate. By taking action and acting like you're courageous, you become courageous. Courage isn't the absence of fear; it's the willingness to confront it head-on. It's about being afraid and doing it anyway.

Sometimes, all it takes is ten seconds of courage—a brief moment to speak up or initiate change. Once you say what needs to be said, you're in the game. Events start taking over that are going to carry you along. All you had to do was initiate. Other times, courage is enduring—a commitment to face challenges and hardships with conviction and belief in a greater purpose. Good people conquer their own fear and take action.

In my own experience, I've encountered moments of intense fear and uncertainty, particularly during difficult business conflicts. I vividly recall a time when a colleague and I were embroiled in a public and contentious dispute. During a phone call with him, my hands were shaking uncontrollably, my heartrate rose, and my face was flushed as adrenaline released throughout my body. This was a fight or flight moment.

> **Life expands and contracts in proportion to your courage.**

It was then that I realized, in the most difficult business conflict of my life, that this is what courage feels like. Despite the fear and discomfort, I realized that courage wasn't about avoiding the sensation of fear but acknowledging it and moving forward anyway. It was a test of endurance. Eventually, we laid aside our differences and made peace with one another.

Moreover, the support and encouragement of those around us can fuel our courage. Just as a friend's reassuring words buoyed my spirits during a challenging time, encouragement from loved ones can provide the heart needed to face our fears. Life expands and contracts in proportion to your courage. When you're afraid, life gets small. But when you are courageous, life expands and becomes big. It's true in both the big and small things. Courage is not an immutable characteristic hidden in our genes. It is a learned behavior, a choice, and a gift.

John

SUBJECT:
Run to the Roar

Dear James,

Learning to be courageous is a gradual process, influenced by our experiences, and choices. Parents play a significant role in shaping their children's courage by instilling in them a confident approach to life. For instance, my son and his wife intentionally encouraged their children to embrace risk, understanding that bumps and bruises are part of their choice. By expecting and accepting these challenges, they raised children who readily face life's uncertainties.

Moreover, courage is cultivated through taking risks and facing the unknown. Each time we step out of our comfort zone and encounter success, we reinforce our courage. Even failures may contribute to our growth, shaping our character and guiding our future decisions. It's like building a muscle—the more we exercise it, the stronger it becomes.

However, courage isn't just an individual endeavor; it's also a gift bestowed upon us by those around us. Encouragement from loved ones provides the heart needed to confront our fears and overcome obstacles. In essence, courage is not merely a personal trait but a collective effort, nurtured by the support and inspiration of others. Encouragement doesn't just mean to praise or lift up someone. It comes from a French word that means "heart." To encourage means to "bring heart" to someone who is lacking it.

Every year I write down the things I learned from that year. I usually discover them by re-reading my journal on New Year's Day. This practice is a much better use of my time than parades and football that don't interest me. The year 2023 was particularly challenging for me. One of the key lessons I learned is embodied in this quote from Dietrich Bonhoeffer: "The Christian needs another Christian who speaks God's Word to him. He needs him again and again when he becomes uncertain and discouraged, for by himself he cannot help himself without belying the truth. . . . The Christ in his own heart is weaker than the Christ in the word of his brother; his own heart is uncertain, his brother's is sure."[37]

This is the very definition of encouragement. We all need it. Our communities of faith depend on it.

Courage, like all virtues, is formed gradually over time. With advancing age, you're much like you were when you were younger, only more so. It is much like the simmering of spaghetti sauce on a stove that over time becomes a more distilled version of itself. Pay attention to your character in your forties and fifties because you are likely to be an exaggerated version of that in your seventies—either to the good or the bad. Courage is a virtue; it's developed over time.

Phillip Brooks wrote, "Some day, in years to come, you will be wrestling with the great temptation, or trembling under the great sorrow of your life. But the real struggle is here, in these quiet weeks. Now it is being decided whether, in the day of your supreme sorrow or temptation, you shall miserably fail or gloriously conquer. Character cannot be made except by a steady, long-continued process."[38]

When I was a young man of twenty-eight years, we lived in Alabama. I played basketball with a guy with whom I went to church. He called me one day and told me he had put my name on an insurance policy so he could win a contest. He asked me to falsely claim ownership of the policy if questioned. So, the auditors called me, and I lied. I felt terrible, but I was confused. I was caught between my friend and telling the truth. I gave in to the pressure.

A couple years later my friend's financial misdeeds became public and were much more pervasive than I knew. It also turned out that he had betrayed his wife. I always wondered if I had blown the whistle when it was a small problem, could it have prevented it from becoming a big problem? I don't know the answer. But that moment formed me ever after. I was not likely to get caught between a friend and the truth. Today I'm going to be on the side of the truth. I'm not going to lie for a friend. How terrible it would be, at the end of your days, to realize that at the heart of all of your decisions wasn't belief, conviction, or desire, but a craving for safety, a desperation for approval, and a deep, deep-seated fear of not being liked.

Paul Assaiante is the squash and tennis coach at Trinity College, where his squash team has won thirteen consecutive national titles. One of his favorite stories is about a pride of lions where the lionesses are the hunters. As they hunt, the oldest lioness is positioned on the far side of the prey. Although she is aged, infirm, and toothless, she has a powerful roar. Whenever the prey hears the roar of the old harmless lioness, they run away from it to their death where the young lionesses are waiting. The moral of the story is that if you run to the roar, you'll usually find that the thing you fear is a toothless, old lioness. Overwhelmingly, the things we most fear never come to pass. We borrow so much trouble with worry.

The solution to most of our anxieties is to run to the roar, not away from it. Often, we find it's not nearly as bad as we imagined. Exclusively thinking of courage as a grand and glorious choice is a mistake. Courage is exercised in both small and great things, but the essence of courage remains the same. Being courageous in smaller things will prepare you for larger challenges. Courage is not about the size of the challenge; it's about confronting our anxieties head-on and realizing that most of what we fear never comes to pass.

Cultivate your courage, and run to the roar.

Courageously yours,
John

SUBJECT:
Congratulations on Your New Leadership Role

Dear James,

As you embark on this new chapter of your career, I want to extend my heartfelt congratulations to you. Taking on the role of a leader requires courage, and I admire your willingness to step up and embrace this challenge.

Throughout our conversations, we've explored the multifaceted nature of courage. It's not merely one of the virtues but rather the essence that infuses every virtue with meaning. Without courage, wisdom remains dormant, and justice lacks a path for application. Courage is what life looks like when we're tested.

I've been continually impressed by the resilience and determination of courageous individuals. They may not always want to act, but they find the strength within themselves to do so anyway. Mental Clarity, I've come to realize, is the child of courage, not the other way around.

Courage manifests itself in various forms and situations. I talked with a former special forces operator who was attending an Ivy League school. You can imagine the abuse he faced from radical professors and their acolytes. He was undeterred. I used to work with an executive vice president of a Fortune 100 company. He was one of the very few men who had been a carrier pilot in the second

> **Courage is what life looks like when we're tested.**

World War from the beginning of the war to the end. His personal courage in tough circumstances was amazing. Whether it's the calm demeanor of a special forces operator facing classroom adversity or the resolve of a WWII fighter pilot navigating the corporate world, courage is forged through life's experiences.

I don't see courage as an intrinsic trait; instead, it is developed over years of making hard choices and sticking to them. My wife often tells our grandkids, "You were made to do hard things." And so they were. And so are you. I've learned that courage isn't reserved for extraordinary feats but is often found in the everyday challenges we encounter. Whether it's a mother anxiously awaiting her child's return home or a woman facing childbirth for the second time, courage is necessary because there is much to fear.

> **You were made to do hard things.**

I knew the headmaster of Christ Covenant School in Nashville who was tragically gunned down by a shooter in 2023. When I heard the news, it was devastating. The situation became even more heart-wrenching as the identities of the other victims were revealed. That day, I wrote in my journal a quote from Tolkien: "The world is indeed full of peril, and in it there are many dark places; but still there is much that is fair, and though in all lands love is now mingled with grief, it grows perhaps the greater."[39]

As you embark on this new journey as a leader, remember that courage is not about the absence of fear, but the willingness to act in spite of it. You will be tested. You may not possess all the courage you will need one day, but you have enough for today. You were made to do hard things!

Truth and Grace,
John

8

Developing Leadership

SYNOPSIS: Alex is a young CFO who is building his team supporting a half billion-dollar company. He came to John asking for help to develop his leadership skills. He aspires one day to run his own company but is still learning what it means to be a leader. He wants to understand the demands of what lies ahead. His three children are all ten or under. He started as an accountant and has grown in his career so far by being really good at his craft. Those around him see his talent. He has good people skills but still thinks of himself as the smart financial guy with good answers.

SUBJECT:
Becoming a Leader

Dear Alex,

I trust this letter finds you well. I wanted to take a moment to follow up on our recent meeting where we discussed your aspirations to develop your leadership skills and eventually start your own company. Your eagerness to grow and your commitment to quality are truly commendable, and I am honored to be a part of your journey toward leadership excellence.

I find ambition to be a wonderful trait. While it gets a bad rap in some circles, the urge to accomplish and build is an inherent human, and perhaps masculine, characteristic. Our culture would be significantly poorer without ambition. Of course, when ambition becomes only about domination and is driven by the desire for applause, it can become unhealthy. Proper ambition is about achieving something good, not about dunking on a competitor or basking in recognition. Good ambition should be celebrated and valued.

The unique role of a leader is to set the direction and help their organization envision a destination. During our conversation, we touched upon the essence of leadership and what it takes to chart a course toward a desired goal. What separates a leader from a manager? Leaders are visionaries—they possess the ability to see beyond the present moment and envision a future that others may not yet perceive. They articulate where they are going and what it will be like when they arrive, inspiring those around them to join the journey.

I was particularly struck by your willingness to explore the invisible world of leadership—the realm of ideas and vision that precedes tangible action. Everything that exists in the visible world first existed in the invisible world. Your company will not exist until you think of it first. The bridge you drove over coming to work today first existed in the designer's imagination before being built across the river. Your ability to cultivate this invisible world within your own mind will undoubtedly shape the future trajectory of your company and inspire those around to join you.

Leaders serve as guides, offering others glimpses into the invisible realm of possibilities. They facilitate the journey from the unseen to the seen, crafting a bridge between vision and reality. Vision is the ability to see the unseen, to envision a future state with clarity and concreteness. The more vividly leaders can imagine this future, the more effectively they can articulate not just the destination, but also the experience of reaching it. This is the essence of leadership.

As we continue to work together to develop your leadership skills, I encourage you to remain focused on the destination—the ultimate goal toward which you are striving. Whether it's five, ten, or twenty years down the road, keep your vision clear. Think about navigating a ship toward some distant spot on the far away shore. You might not land at that precise point, but you must have the point to steer toward.

I often remember Admiral James Stockdale, a highly decorated US Navy officer and aviator, who spent time as a prisoner of war (POW) in North Vietnam at the infamous "Hanoi Hilton." Throughout his imprisonment, he had unwavering certainty about his ultimate rescue, even in the face of great adversity. I hope that you too can find that clarity and determination in your leadership journey.

Your ambition is a strength, and I celebrate it. Remember, your leadership is for the benefit of others. Keep striving toward your goals with integrity and vision. I have no doubt you will achieve great things.

Truth and Grace,
John

SUBJECT:
Building Championship Teams

Dear Alex,

I hope this email finds you well after our recent discussion on leadership at the conference. Your eagerness to delve into the intricacies of leadership is truly commendable, and I'm excited to continue exploring this journey with you.

One key takeaway from our conversation is the pivotal role of attracting exceptional individuals to your team. As you correctly observed, championships are indeed won in the draft, not just in the playbook. Abby Wambach, former leader of the US National Women's Soccer Team and the Women's soccer coach at the University of California (Cal), observed that "athletes win athletic competitions."[40] At one level it's a glimpse of the obvious but it's a clear reminder that there is no substitute in athletics for being big, fast, and strong. The higher the level of competition, the more that's true. It's clear that the caliber of individuals you surround yourself with can profoundly influence your organization's success.

Leadership, at its core, involves positioning your organization for success in a dynamic and ever-evolving landscape. Assembling the right team is paramount to this endeavor. Great leaders draw great people toward them. Remember the wisdom referenced by Stetson Bennett, the great football philosopher and natty-winning quarterback from Georgia: "It isn't the X's and O's, it's the Jimmy's and the Joe's."[41] What he meant is that football is all about the players—— not the plays they run. Likewise, in business, your ability to envision a future state and gather the right people to bring that vision to life are keys to success.

Reflecting on hiring decisions, it's crucial to prioritize potential and capability over immediate fit. While the safe option may seem appealing, individuals with untapped potential often possess a higher ceiling for growth and innovation. As leaders, we must be willing to take calculated risks and invest in talent that can drive long-term success.

> **Great leaders draw great people toward them.**

As you said, championships are won in the draft. The foundation of great companies lies in the selection process. Bill Gates emphasized the critical role of top talent, stating that without the top twenty-five individuals at Microsoft, the company would have been just ordinary.[42] During that period, Microsoft's price-to-earnings ratio (PE) was over ten points higher than that of an average company, highlighting the billions of dollars of shareholder value created by these top performers. This illustrates a universal truth: a few outstanding individuals consistently generate disproportionate value within any organization.

We can all understand the need to attract great performers to the team, but the question is how. It's crucial to offer the right deal and the right job for a great person, but even more important is the relationship between the two of you. Your best people are a volunteer army, and you want them showing up every day. This typically happens because they believe in your vision and trust you. Never downplay the personal dimension of attracting the best people.

Additionally, it's essential to recognize the dichotomy between perception and reality in leadership. As the boss, everybody wants to present their best self. But in reality, they are a tuxedo in the front and a hospital gown in the back. You can strive to put your best foot forward, but those around you are always going to be able to see you from the back. They will see your failures and mistakes—the ways you're kind of flapping in the breeze. You just have to get comfortable with people seeing behind the curtain and acknowledging your imperfections.

Embracing uncertainty is a hallmark of effective leadership. Just as March Madness brackets can't predict every outcome, leaders must accept that ambiguity is inherent in decision-making. While groups may seek consensus, true leadership pursues the best possible outcome.

In our journey to becoming better leaders, let's continue to explore these principles and apply them to our roles. I look forward to our ongoing discussions and the insights they will bring.

Truth and Grace,
John

SUBJECT:
Maintaining Composure in Conflict

Dear Alex,

I'm sorry to hear about the battle you are facing at work. Navigating difficult situations as a leader requires a delicate balance between addressing the issue at hand and maintaining composure. One of my hard-won principles is this: don't become the issue. It's crucial not to let emotions push you into behavior where you become the issue instead of the other fellow. Heaven knows I learned this the hard way.

Don't become the issue.

I recall a moment early in my career when I allowed anger to get the best of me. I was coaching Babe Ruth baseball, and the umpire made a terrible call. I lashed out impulsively, kicking a folding chair in frustration. Instead of serving as a physical sign of my frustration, the chair folded up perfectly and sailed over the fence into the crowd of parents. I had to climb the fence and sheepishly retrieve the chair. All eyes were on the spectacle of my foolishness. They all forgot about the umps terrible call. However, from that incident, I learned a valuable lesson about managing my emotions in conflict.

This formulation of the purpose of business is biblical. It's clear and easily understood, even though its application is infinitely variable. I like this definition because it applies to all people in all places at all times. It's as relevant today as it was in 524 or will be in 2824. It works for interns and CEO's. It's as useful in Zambia or New York City.

Luther was careful not to allow loving our neighbor to become a religious work. He said "God has no need of our good works but our neighbor does". Those good works include sharing the gospel, being generous with our resources, caring for people and much more.

Recently, there was a man who behaved very poorly, damaging one of my good friends. I was sorely tempted to react impulsively and indulge my predilection for extravagant action. Instead, I sought counsel from a trusted friend who advised a more measured approach. By quietly engaging in the background and addressing the issue quietly, I was able to resolve the conflict. I maintained control of the situation and prevented myself from becoming the center of attention. I wish I were always that self-possessed.

In challenging moments, it's essential to remember that losing your temper rarely achieves positive outcomes. Our family motto, "The louder they are, the dumber they are," underscores the wisdom of keeping a level head and your mouth shut. Those who resort to shouting and aggression often lack the intelligence to resolve conflicts effectively. As a leader, it's imperative to manage yourself and avoid being drawn into unnecessary confrontations. At a more spiritual level, the anger of man does not accomplish the righteousness of God. No matter how tempted we are to display and act in anger, it's a terrible danger.

Moving forward, I encourage you to approach conflicts with a calm and composed demeanor. Doing so will be much easier if your identity is not wrapped up in the matter at hand. The conflict is just a conflict; it's not a battle for your identity. Focus on addressing the issue rather than being driven by your emotions. Your emotions are temporary states, intended to provide depth and joy to life and to motivate action. They tend to change quickly. It's okay to acknowledge what you are feeling, but your actions should be driven by your values, commitments, and interests. By doing so, you'll demonstrate strong leadership and maintain the respect of those around you.

Truth and Grace,
John

SUBJECT:
Nurturing Strategic Vision and Organizational Culture

Dear Alex,

I hope this email finds you well. We have been discussing strategy and culture, and I believe they are linked. Strategy is often an overblown topic in business, but conceptually, it's quite simple. It's a general approach to solving a problem or capitalizing on a situation.

Let's start with the analogy of strategies being akin to torpedoes. Much like a cheesy World War II movie where a submarine captain fires torpedoes at enemy ships, as leaders, we must strategically launch a limited number of initiatives into the unseen future. Some of these strategies will hit their targets and bring success, while others may miss. However, the essence lies in our ability to make calculated bets on the actions that will propel us towardtowards our desired future state. Just like the submarine captain, we can only make a few critical bets, so we must make them count.

It's important to ask yourself from time to time, "Where are my bets?" Always ensure you have some strategic initiatives in play. Indeed, the hallmark of effective leadership is the capacity to envision the future environment and devise strategies to succeed in that future state. This involves placing strategic bets on initiatives that have the potential to drive meaningful change in the business landscape. As leaders, we must continuously assess and refine our strategic approach, recognizing that not all bets will yield the desired outcomes.

Moreover, I want to emphasize the critical role of organizational culture in shaping the collective identity and behaviors within a company. Culture, as I describe it, is the imagined community that binds individuals together in pursuit of common goals. Leaders play a pivotal role in fostering this sense of community by articulating shared vision, values, and norms.

Culture is not merely a set of policies or guidelines but rather a deeply ingrained set of behaviors and attitudes that define how things are done within an organization. As leaders, it's imperative that we uphold and reinforce the desired culture by setting clear expectations and addressing behaviors that deviate from these standards.

I liken culture to the margin of acceptability within an organization. What we tolerate ultimately defines the boundaries of our culture. As leaders, we must be vigilant in maintaining a healthy culture that aligns with our values and objectives, recognizing that culture permeates every aspect of organizational life.

I look forward to continuing our discussions on these important topics and exploring how we can further enhance your leadership capabilities.

Truth and Grace,
John

SUBJECT:
Key Priorities for Building a Successful Business

Hi Alex,

I love your ideas about starting a new business. You certainly have the capabilities to succeed. You asked a great question: Where do I focus first? I have some thoughts for you.

There are three primary priorities in business, which should be addressed in this order: control, profitability, and growth. Getting these out of order can be perilous.

1 CONTROL

Control means the business consistently operates as you intend it to. This involves satisfying customers at a predictable cost and being able to forecast financial results with reasonable accuracy. It's about having processes and systems in place. In theory, this might be called achieving product/market fit, but control also implies predictability.

Prominent business executive and investor Cam Lanier once told me, "You have an investable business when there is a linear relationship between the application of resources and generating revenue." He was talking about control.

> **Revenue is vanity.**
>
> **Earnings are sanity.**
>
> **Cash is reality.**

2 PROFITABILITY

Profitability is crucial because, until you achieve it, your business is consuming cash. A business consuming cash is on a runway that will eventually run out, leading to a crash if it doesn't become airborne. Businesses are not naturally profitable; they must be taught to be so. Achieving even a small profit is better than losing money, but businesses operating on razor-thin margins are vulnerable to unforeseen events.

I like to say that: Revenue is vanity. Earnings are sanity. Cash is reality.

Profit measures the value your business creates after accounting for the cost of all inputs. A small profit indicates low value creation, while a large profit shows high value creation. Never apologize for being profitable. Running a high-margin business is much more enjoyable and sustainable than running one on low margins.

Some industries inherently have low profitability due to factors like fragmented competition and low barriers to entry. It's challenging to build a great business in a bad industry. Even once achieved, profitability must be defended constantly as the market and competitors will work to commodify your business, nibbling away your profits.

3 GROWTH

Growth is exciting and creates opportunities but comes with risks. Some resist growth, preferring comfort over the risk inherent in expansion. However, growth is vital. Living things grow; static entities, like rocks, do not. Without growth, competitors will eventually surpass and challenge your core business.

Trying to grow a business without control leads to a mess and damages your brand. Attempting to grow without profitability often results in running out of cash.

Growth can only precede profitability if two conditions are met: a very large addressable market and an ample supply of inexpensive and patient capital. Only a minority of businesses meet these criteria.

In the long term, pursuing opportunities is more profitable than merely solving problems. Fixing problems only returns you to your previous state, while pursuing opportunities propels you forward. Despite the risks, prioritizing growth is key to long-term success.

I hope these insights help you prioritize your efforts effectively. Best of luck with your new venture!

Regards,
John

SUBJECT:
Unleashing Your Leadership Potential

Dear Alex,

As you continue on your journey to develop your leadership skills and make a meaningful impact within your organization, I wanted to share some insights and advice that I believe will be instrumental in unlocking your full potential.

First and foremost, it's crucial to tell yourself the truth about your strengths as a leader. While your background as a public accountant has undoubtedly served you well, your greatest asset lies in your ability to rally people around a common objective and drive results. You have a unique talent for inspiring others to row in the same direction and achieve shared goals. It's time to put your energy into this leadership skill, relegating accounting tasks to others. Your functional accounting skills got you here but are not your future.

I understand that stepping away from the comfort of numbers and financial statements may feel daunting, but I want to remind you of your past successes and experiences that demonstrate your innate leadership abilities. Think back to your days as a pitcher, standing on the mound with the weight of the game resting on your shoulders. You enjoyed that moment and were good at it. Now, it's time to channel that same courage and determination into your role as a leader within your organization. The comfort zone is a death trap.

Moreover, every leader needs a support system of individuals who believe in their capabilities and provide unwavering encouragement. Whether it's a mentor, a friend, or a colleague, having someone in your corner who stands behind you and believes in your potential can make all the difference.

An inspiring example of the power of belief is exemplified by my son-in-law, who came to America from Korea as a young boy. Upon his arrival, he faced the daunting challenge of not speaking English, yet his kindergarten teacher recognized his potential and took him under her wing. Every day after school, she taught him English, a gesture that would profoundly impact his life. He flourished academically and eventually became the valedictorian of his high school. Her belief in him changed his life. All good leaders have people in their corner, providing help and confidence at critical moments.

I have full confidence in your ability to lead with distinction and make a significant impact within your organization. Embrace your unique strengths, draw upon your past experiences, and surround yourself with supporters who believe in your potential. God made you to make a difference. Go make it.

Truth and Grace,
John

9

Living With Courage

 **SYNOPSIS:** In this final chapter, John discusses leadership in his personal life during a very stressful and emotional season.

SUBJECT:
An Unexpected Storm

Dear Grandkids,

I want to share a story that you might already know a little about, but I want to give you a glimpse of what was happening behind the scenes. I want you to understand how your grandmother, Happy, and I navigated this journey, our thought processes, our hopes, and the decisions we made in an unexpected storm in our lives.

In April of 2022, we celebrated Aunt Katie's birthday with lunch at the Battery with her family. We enjoyed the barbecue and had a wonderful time. The next day was Easter Sunday. As the afternoon wore on, my stomach began to ache. Monday it progressed and the pain worsened, prompting a visit to urgent care. They quickly sent me to the hospital, where doctors discovered a bowel obstruction that they believed to be a tumor.

On Wednesday of that week, a surgeon, who seemed to be a miraculous provision in our life, removed the tumor along with eight inches of my colon. The doctors then started me on a six-month course of chemo, which concluded in November of 2022. While we were aware of the possibility of the cancer returning, it felt theoretical. I underwent chemo treatment for stage three cancer. It seemed serious, but we believed it might be over.

The scans in December of that year were clear, as were the scans in April of the following year. When we did the third set of scans in July of 2023, they initially told me the results were clear too. But on Tuesday, my surgical oncologist called to inform me that radiology had made a mistake, and my cancer had returned. I was shocked and understandably reeling. How could we go from "all clear" to "not so fast" in less than twenty-four hours? Happy and I decided not to talk about this until we saw my oncologist. The next day, my oncologist called again and scheduled an appointment. As you can tell it was all moving very quickly. So, on Thursday, Happy and I went to his office. While there, he told us that I had inoperable and incurable stage four colon cancer. He told us he would be focusing on treatments that might extend my life.

We had suspected this possibility, but hearing the diagnosis spoken out loud was a heavy blow. We weren't truly prepared for the news– no one ever is. The fear and uncertainty about what my diagnosis meant were overwhelming. One of my first thoughts was about having to call my daughters, Katie and Claire, to tell them. How do you have that conversation? I remembered that it required just ten seconds of courage. So, once they were on the phone and I said the first sentence or two, events took over.

Uncle Thomas, and his family were on a trip to London. Not wanting to disrupt their vacation, I delayed telling them until early the next week. I eventually caught him at the airport on his way home and broke the news.

I never imagined having to tell my children something like this. The weight of it was enormous and extremely difficult. Quite suddenly, we found ourselves having to tell our family about this disease that could likely take my life. While I am secure in God's promises of eternal life, the prospect of having to say goodbye to Martha, our children, and each of you seemed more than I could bear. We were scrambling to find solid footing for how we would live in the face of our new reality.

So, the next weekend, Happy and I borrowed a friend's home in the mountains and took a long weekend away. As is my habit when I need to think carefully about something, I developed a list of twenty-eight questions to work through while we were there. That weekend, we didn't get through all of them, but having them in front of us helped us focus. Some of these questions were "me" questions, but many were "we" questions for both of us. It was during that weekend that we began to formulate the answer to the question of how shall I now live. Faced with a medical reality that had created an expiration date, we had to learn to live with that reality. How could we possibly do that?

I don't know when you will read these words. I suspect it will be after I have already gone to heaven. I am writing this during the good days, before the symptoms of cancer begin to show. In the next few emails, I want to share a bit about how we navigated this challenging time. I want you to know that you can rely on God to be with you too. Courage is definitely required, but remember, you have the creator of courage on your side.

Remember, you have the creator of courage on your side.

Love you always,
Pops

SUBJECT:
Questions

Dear Grandkids,

You might be wondering about the questions we explored during our weekend in the mountains, so I thought I would share them along with the story of that time. Here were the questions we delved into:

Questions In The Face of Inoperable Stage Four Cancer:

- How is God calling me?
- What might we regret at the end of it?
- How do I balance the work I love and feel called to with my desire to spend more time with family?
- How is Satan tempting me?
- What does living well look like in this season of life?
- How do I give Martha more of a voice in deciding?
- How do Martha and I develop more intimacy?
- How can Martha and I make this a "we" season?
- How do I deal with the fear of this going by so quickly?
- How do I make this about living, not about dying?
- What should I do about working?
- How shall we then live?
- How can I use my platform wisely?
- How do I keep stage four cancer from becoming my identity?
- How will I cope with the process of dying?
- Will my friends and others stand with me?

- Does my 70th birthday celebration this year matter?
- Are there things I should cut out of my life?
- What is the right timing for decisions and communication?
- What changes should I make to better cope with chemo?
- How can I prepare to die without shifting my focus away from living well?
- What actions will I take to make chemo a lifestyle?
- Where is the battle?
- How long do I have?
- How open should I be about how and what I feel?
- How open should I be about including others in this journey?
- How do I fight the battle of eating a Mediterranean diet since I am going to have to eat food I don't like?
- How do I maintain or improve my fitness?

Over the weekend, we diligently worked through these questions. It was stormy when we arrived on Friday, so we took the opportunity to dive deep into our list, dedicating the entire day to reflection and discussion. We had dinner plans that evening, which provided a nice break. Saturday greeted us with beautiful weather, allowing us to enjoy time at the lake, play pickleball, go for a hike, and have another lovely dinner (a gift from my mentees). Most of the hard work was accomplished on Friday, and we spent the rest of the weekend enjoying ourselves in the mountains.

These questions were essential for processing our situation. "How is God calling me?" was particularly significant as I feared potential regrets at the end of my life. By envisioning the finish line and working backward, we identified what actions to take and what to avoid. Balancing the work I love and feel called to with my desire to spend more time with family was another critical consideration. I often deferred major questions to Happy, seeking her thoughts and perspectives.

I wanted to make this a "we" season with Happy, ensuring that we faced everything together. We also had to confront the fear of how quickly things might progress. Many patients with the same genetic mutation in their tumors as mine don't survive beyond the first year after their cancer returns. If we had asked the doctor then, "How long do I have?" the answer would likely have been, "About a year." We needed to figure out how to focus on living, not dying, and how to use our platform wisely.

We pondered how to keep stage four cancer from consuming all our attention, what parts of life to cut out, the right timing for decisions, and what changes to make to cope better with chemo. Preparing to die without losing focus on living well was another challenging aspect. We also discussed how open we should be about our experience and the importance of including others in this journey.

Though we had twenty-eight questions, we only got through ten. Once we addressed the initial questions, the rest seemed less critical. We talked about the reality of our deaths and that we are made for eternity, not immortality. Stage four cancer made me more aware of my expiration date, but it's just as real for everyone else.

I realized my emotions were like two hands: in my left hand were fear, sadness, resentment, anger, and uncertainty; in my right hand were thankfulness, love, peace, and trust. At any moment, I could choose which hand to live out of. Initially, I lived more out of my left hand, but over time, I spent less and less time there. I don't see the negative emotions in my left hand as weaknesses or wrong; they're simply part of being human. It's natural to feel fear and sadness when facing a death sentence. However, you have the power to react based on your values, commitments, and core beliefs rather than just your feelings.

Anger is a particularly interesting emotion. I have this idea that anger is synthetic. You feel anger when you don't want to feel what is lying behind that anger. Anger is a "safer" emotion to experience. It's worth it to dig down to find out what is behind the anger. We found

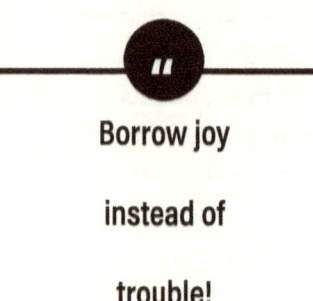

Borrow joy

instead of

trouble!

betrayal, shame, regret, and deep sorrow. The journey down is always worth it.

We can borrow trouble from the future, and it might happen or it might not. Borrowing trouble robs us of today's pleasures. Conversely, borrowing joy from the future is certain. Living in anticipation of a joyful future is much more fulfilling than worrying about uncertain troubles. Borrow joy instead of trouble!

I hope this gives you some insight into our weekend of questions and how we navigated this challenging time. I'll share more in the next email.

Love always,
Pops

SUBJECT:
Living Gloriously

Dear Grandkids,

At my nephew Steven's wedding, they played a song by David Wilcox called "All the Roots Grow Deeper When It's Dry."[43] This song stuck with me because it captures a profound truth: in difficult or dry seasons, our roots must go deeper in search of water. Hard times can be the richest times. What we superficially call "good" or "bad" are inherently bound together and inseparable. When you get one, you get the other. Our roots into our relationship with God push deeper into the soil, urgently searching for living water. Our roots into friends and family also push deeper, past superficial things into "truer" things. We become aware of our needs. Being aware of life's brevity is a good thing. When you have an expiration date, greens get greener, blues get bluer, and memories become more vivid. It might be more helpful to describe events as easy or hard rather than labeling them as good or bad.

Happy and I are more open, intentional, and intimate together. As a couple, we don't spend all of our days talking about cancer or dying, but we do talk about it sometimes. We also talk about our children, grandchildren, and all the other important aspects of our life. In the beginning, we talked about living well. We have since changed that language to "living gloriously." This change came from something Happy said about not wasting the good days. I feel good right now. Although I have less stamina, more weakness, and less hair—those are all consequences of chemo—these days are good because I am asymptomatic with respect to my cancer. These times won't last forever, but they are good days. We want to live these days gloriously.

So I ask myself, what does living gloriously look like? There are four elements that are essential to living gloriously.

1 **AWARENESS OF GLORY AND BEAUTY:** Our hearts are drawn to beauty. Beauty is healing and inspires wonder. A friend from church who also has cancer said that when she was diagnosed, it was as if the world became technicolor. She became so much more aware of its beauty and often found it in unexpected places.

2 **DEEP CONNECTION WITH GOD AND EACH OTHER:** Christianity is an individual decision but a team sport. We've come to deeply value our community. Relationships—with our family

and community—are the fuel for the journey. They're what makes life rich and full. Living gloriously is living with an awareness and a pursuit of the relationships around you–first with God, second with Happy, third with my family, and fourth with my friends.

3 **LIVING AT PEACE:** There's an inherent relationship between trust and peace; one flows from the other. This year has been difficult knowing that I have brought sadness to others. Cancer creates turmoil for my wife, children, and grandchildren. All of them have been unwittingly dragged into this. Cancer wasn't their plan either. I realized that I was taking too much responsibility for that. I have concluded that love and sorrow are always connected to each other. When we choose to love, we are signing up for sorrow, whether we know it or not. All our loves will end one day, one way or the other. When we fell in love and chose to get married, we signed up for the fact that one day death would separate us. It's actually in our vow that these vows only last until we're parted by death. Gordon McDonald reflected on turning eighty and talked about the importance of preparing your heart for obscurity.[44] As you age or get sick, you become less and less relevant. The ultimate obscurity is death. You must prepare yourself for that because one day you'll pass away. That's just a reality.

4 **LIVING ON PURPOSE:** Don't fritter your life away with things that aren't going to matter. Live aligned with your purpose. Happy and I developed this statement that our purpose is "to invest in the next generation to the glory of God." The idea came from her because she's much wiser than I am. This idea applies to our children and grandchildren. It even extends

to the great-grandchildren that haven't been born yet. It also extends to the younger men and women that we mentor and befriend. Living gloriously is living on purpose with a mind for some greater things.

I hope these reflections inspire you as much as they have inspired me. Life's sorrows and joys are interwoven, and it's in embracing both that we live gloriously.

Love always,
Pops

SUBJECT:
Embracing the Journey

Dear Grandkids,

During our weekend getaway, one of the pivotal questions we asked ourselves was, "Do we want to spend the good times taking trips?" We have the financial resources to travel the world and could easily make a list of all the places we want to visit. However, we both decided that while there are still things we'd like to do, we don't want to spend our good times on overseas trips. We're grateful for the trips we've taken and might take more in the future, but that's not our antidote for impending pain. Instead, we want to spend the good times with people and be fully aware of what God has called us to do in this season. Glorious living is more important to us than checking off a bucket list.

Happy just signed up for another year of mentoring and continues to participate in new activities. She is preparing for a big teaching day at our church next February. She's not putting her life on hold, and neither am I. I am glad that, so far, I have been able to maintain a pretty full schedule. There are days when I can't do everything I want to do, and I have to learn from that. God made us for good works, which he prepared for us beforehand (Ephesians 2:10, NIV).

Frederick Buechner is an American author and theologian. He wrote something that has come to seem profoundly true in this season of life: "Listen to your life. See it for the fathomless mystery it is. In the boredom and pain of it, no less than in the excitement and gladness: touch, taste, smell your way to the holy and hidden heart of it, because in the last analysis all moments are glorious moments, and life itself is grace."[45]

Recently, the doctor noticed something concerning and accelerated my scans. I was very nervous, knowing that at some point, the therapy would fail and the cancer would accelerate its growth. This created anxiety and put me back in my left hand of fear and worry. The night before the scans, I came across the idea that if God picked this road for me, it's a good road. There's a lot of submission and trust in that statement. It wasn't easy to accept, but I believe it's true. Embracing this gave me peace. The scans didn't show anything new, but from that moment, I felt a deep sense of peace, believing that this is God's gift to me. God grants me peace so that I'm not in turmoil.

This journey has been incredibly hard for Happy. There are so many emotions at play: sorrow, sadness, regret for future experiences we may miss together, anxiety about carving out a life alone, and the uncertainty of what that life looks like. Honestly, I think it is harder for her than it is for me. Somewhere in the middle of this process, I will be gone to heaven, leaving her and my family to manage the aftermath of my death. It always works like that; they have the hard part. I think about this and feel guilty.

There are swirling emotions that are incredibly difficult to deal with, and we often talk about them together. Happy has found a book called *Dark Clouds, Deep Mercy* to be deeply helpful.[46] It explores the biblical concept of lament and how we can openly present our grievances to God in the most direct manner possible. The book encourages us to be honest about our emotions and bring our complaints to God, who in turn helps us find peace. It focuses on a biblical pattern of lament, highlighting that many Psalms are laments where the psalmists ask God, "How long will you let these people oppress me?" (Psalm 13:1, NIV). These prayers are very direct and emotional, but through them, God provides healing in the midst of our struggles. While God doesn't always resolve the issue immediately, he brings us back to his character, where the psalmists ultimately find peace. As have we.

I write these because I want you to know what has happened. Even more, I hope that our experiences will offer you valuable insights and will serve you well.

Love always,
Pops

SUBJECT:
The Power of Thankfulness

Dear Grandkids,

During the global pandemic of 2020, faced with many days of confinement, Happy and I developed a routine to do something different every day. With the days blending together, we found it essential to break the monotony. For instance, on Mondays, we would take a walk we hadn't taken before. On Fridays, we would have a celebration dinner where we reviewed the things from the preceding week for which we were thankful.

Our celebration dinners are the only structure that survived the pandemic. Almost every Friday, we recount together what we are thankful for from the previouspreceding week. We almost always come up with a long list of things that bend our hearts in a new way as we head into the weekend. Sometimes, we'll have a glass of wine and then do it over dinner. In cold weather, we sit by the fire pit, and in warmer weather, we may be out on the porch. We always find someplace comfortable and relaxing so we can celebrate. We try not to veer too far off from this and talk of other things. We just focus on what we have to celebrate.

I have trained myself to say "thankful" instead of "grateful." In the English language, we are grateful "for" something, but we are thankful "to" someone. Gratefulness is an unfocused word; thankfulness is focused on the giver of the gift. I'm thankful to God for the breath I take every day. Thankfulness is a word and emotion that provokes humility because I have to be thankful to someone. Gratefulness requires no humility on my part. Both are expressions of appreciation, but thankfulness inclines my heart toward humility for the person who did something for me or for my Heavenly Father who did everything for me.

> **Thankfulness is focused on the giver of the gift.**

A friend visits me every afternoon after my chemo when I am feeling weird and strange. I am thankful to him and humbled by his deeply personal expression of goodness and affection. I've been on this thankful vs. grateful kick long enough that I'm very aware that the people around me have almost abandoned the word thankfulness in favor of gratitude.

I try to always stay thankful. Thankfulness is an important element of dealing with cancer and chemo. It is my way of being acultural, not anti-cultural.

Remember, in all things, to be thankful.

Love you always,
Pops

SUBJECT:
Facing the Reality of Death

Dear Grandkids,

I hope this email finds you well. I want to share a remarkable time from 2022 that strengthened my faith and gave me a profound conviction about life and death.

When I was in the hospital in 2022, two doctors provided by the hospital proposed surgery for me. Tuesday night, after they messed up my pain medication, I began to think clearly for the first time. I felt awful but began to see that their incompetence might kill me. After praying about it, I resolved to take control of my health and my own care.

So, as if it was an answer to my prayer, the next morning, a woman walked into my room and introduced herself as Kate, my surgeon. She had been called by the husband of one of the women in Happy's Bible study and asked to take on my case as a personal favor. I did not know the man who asked Kate to come help me. He did not know me from anyone. But the next morning at eight o'clock, Kate was in my room discussing my surgery.

At first, I was very direct with her. After all, I had decided to be completely in charge of my health care decisions. It's kind of funny actually. The moment I decided to be in charge, my Heavenly Father took over. I did not see it coming. I asked her when she proposed to do the surgery. She said she would do it at noon that day, and that's exactly what she did. It was wonderful and miraculous for me to have her show up and help me take over my own care.

The surgery was on Wednesday, and by Friday, I felt better and had visitors. However, on Friday at about eleven, when I got up from my bed to go to the bathroom, I fell over and coded. I was gone.

Happy later told me that it was like a medical drama. All of a sudden, the room was full of people yelling and screaming, using words like "stat" and "epinephrine." In the midst of that chaos, Happy went to the corner of the room and prayed. She knew I wasn't there. They got out the paddles and shocked me back to life. She said she had an out-of-body experience where she floated above the chaos of the room watching.

When I came back, I had no idea what had happened. I only realized it later. Happy was there, whispering in my ear that everything was going to be fine. I spent the next several days in a critical care bed. During that time, I faced the real possibility of my death. But, in the face of death, I realized that my faith in Jesus was secure. It was not a hospital conversation. Instead it was an awareness that my faith is a settled hope.

I don't love the phrase "you never know" because it implies permission to abandon our core beliefs under pressure. However, in this case, I couldn't be certain until I faced the imminent possibility of death. Because of God's grace, I knew I would live forever. I came away from that experience with a clear conviction that this matter was settled. This experience was transformative for both Happy and me. It strengthened our faith and brought us even closer together.

I want you to know that God is always trustworthy. He always cares for you. He is the reason for our hope.

Love,
Pops

SUBJECT:
Trusting God Through Life's Challenges

Dear Grandkids,

I want to share with you some personal reflections from the past three years. As you might imagine a lot has happened, and I feel like I have learned and grown immensely

In the summer of 2021, I took a sabbatical and spent some time at the beach, trying to determine, among other things, how long I would continue working. After much thought and prayer, I concluded that there will come a time when I can no longer work, but not today. This realization has served me well.

This line of thinking works in a number of ways as there will be a future outcome, but we cannot know when it will arrive. I can hold this present moment with an open hand knowing that it won't last forever. But, and this is important, I don't have to borrow that future moment into the present. I can live in the present with the callings and capacities I have today.

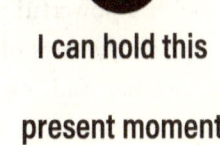

I can hold this present moment with an open hand.

During 2020, I lost two very significant people who acted as shepherds in my life. A shepherd is someone who is deeply engaged with you and watches out for your spiritual and personal well being. My dear friend Regi, who was a shepherd for me, passed away in January. By the end of that year, my sister, who was also my shepherd, was diagnosed with dementia. Her family decided to move her to St. Augustine so that Carter and his family would be able to watch over her care. Both of the people who functioned as my shepherd were gone. These losses left me feeling angry and bereft. In my heart I demanded that someone else would step up and fill that role.

During my sabbatical, I received a clear answer from God: Stop it! Give up this demand for a shepherd. God is the only shepherd you will ever have. He is all you will need. Since then, I have spent the last three years deeply studying the 23rd Psalm. The first line, "The LORD is my shepherd," is particularly profound. In Hebrew, the word for "Lord" is the holy name of God, a name so sacred that vowels were omitted, and it was not pronounced. David was emphasizing that the God of the universe is my personal shepherd. Then comes the words, "I shall not want." There is a good argument that these words could be, "What else could I want?" Put together, Because the holy God of the universe has decided to be my shepherd, I have no need of more.

The linguistic centerpiece of the 23rd Psalm is "For Thou art with me." This phrase stands at the center, with an equal number of phrases before and after it. Obviously it's no accident. This phrase is the heart of the Psalm, emphasizing God's presence with us. The Psalm ends with a powerful promise: "Surely goodness and mercy shall follow me all the days of my life." The word "follow" is better translated as "pursue," and "mercy" as "compassion," akin to a mother's love for her yet unborn child. David describes how God pursues us with relentless mercy and compassion.

In 2023 I realized that my demand for a shepherd the previous year was God's calling to be one. Rather than resenting what I thought I lacked, God was calling me to be more intentional in watching out for the spiritual and personal well being of specific people in my life.

God went before us in the summer of 2021 preparing us for what lay ahead in 2022. Without the insights gained from the sabbatical, my health challenges would have been infinitely more difficult to handle.

After the cancer came back in 2022, I recognized the possibility of becoming depressed. I have a history of depression so I know what it feels like. (I bet you didn't know that about me.) In this case, I felt I was walking near the pit but hadn't fallen in. I told Martha that if I became depressed, everything would become exponentially more difficult. So, I sought out a counselor. A dear friend found a capable, highly educated woman about my age.

I told the counselor I wanted to ensure I was addressing my problems and not hiding from them. We met for six to eight months, but there was a significant difference in our faith perspectives. My comfort and confidence in facing cancer are deeply rooted in my faith in Jesus Christ, not in cognitive behavioral therapy.

In one of our sessions, she shared a quote from St. Augustine: "Love God and do as you please."[47] While this is indeed accurate, the other half of that quote is "for a heart so trained by love will not do anything to offend its beloved." Together, these sentences convey a much deeper meaning than the first one alone. This exchange helped me realize that she was not the right counselor for me. Perhaps I need a pastor more than I need a shrink. In our final session together, she acknowledged that throughout our time together, she had never seen me shy away from the truth. I appreciated the kindness of her recognition. If I were to hire another counselor, I would start by admitting that my comfort comes from my faith in Jesus, not psychotherapy.

I have always found God to be trustworthy. I hope you will.

Love always,
Pops

SUBJECT:
Living Authentically

Dear Grandkids,

Happy and I discovered that, due to my health circumstances, our voices have become louder. People are inevitably looking at us and wondering, "What's going on with them?" I am aware of this but I am cautious too. I don't want to present a cleaned up image of my relationship with God; I want to be honest. I am not packaging my story for public consumption to lead an audience to a conclusion. I've made a conscious decision to live out my cancer journey openly. I know people will watch and perhaps benefit from our story. Some of us withdraw when we get sick. While there is a legitimate self-protectiveness in that approach, it deprives others of the benefit of our experience.

I have invited those close to me into this process. Every Monday morning at 8 o'clock, I send a note to the men I will talk with that week, updating them on my health. This helps us spend less time discussing my health during our meetings. While I know they care, I also understand they hire me to help them. I am committed to openly answering any questions they have, but I don't want to use all our time together to only talk take up our time together talking about my health.

Living openly with cancer is a gift I can give to others. Most people don't experience this. My openness might help them when they face a similar journey with someone close to them or when it's their turn. It's an important part of our shared experience. I hope you, my children and grandchildren, will come to understand and appreciate this as part of your own journey too. Throughout this process, I strive to be authentic without being performative.

Vulnerability means being open about your brokenness. Dietrich Bonhoeffer, in his book *Life Together,* says, "In confession the breakthrough to community takes place. Sin demands to have a man by himself. It withdraws him from the community. The more isolated a person is, the more destructive will be the power of sin over him and the more deeply he becomes involved in it, the more disastrous is his isolation."[48] I need to share my life with others for their good. But, let's be clear, I need to share this journey with others for my protection too. The trick is knowing how deeply to share with a particular group of people. You can certainly overshare. I have decided to err on the side of honesty, knowing that there will be only a few people who need to know the last five percent.

I want to encourage you, to live openly and fearlessly. Don't be afraid to show your true selves to those you trust. Embrace vulnerability, and let it build deeper connections with the people around you. Be brave in sharing your journey, it will serve them and protect you. Courage will be required, but God himself will make up anything you lack.

Be brave in sharing your journey.

Love,
Pops

SUBJECT:
A Final Message from Pops

Dear Grandchildren,

Over the past few months, we've often approached the question of my long-term prognosis but stopped short of asking the doctors outright. We didn't want to know the answer. You're either about the business of living or about the business of dying, and we didn't want to borrow that worry until it was unavoidable. However, during our last set of scans, as the tumors had grown again, Dr. French mentioned the need for me to enroll in a clinical trial at Vanderbilt. This discussion led me to finally ask the question, "Dr. French, how long do I have left?"

Doctors provide a statistical prognosis based on extensive knowledge and experience. I've learned that doctors understand ten thousand times more about what's going on inside me than I do, but they don't know everything. There are still vast mysteries within the human body. This doesn't negate their knowledge, but it does remind us that they are not omniscient. A leading cardiologist once said that the medical community understands about sixty percent of what happens inside the human heart. There is still much we don't know.

I am reminded that I must balance two perspectives. The first box contains medicine and the scientific understanding of cause and effect in a closed system. I accept that reality and can see that my death is the most likely outcome of this cancer journey. The second box also holds the uniformity of cause and effect, but it's an open system. God is not powerless—even in the face of cancer. Although he doesn't promise to heal my cancer, he has done so before. But my belief in God does not hang on whether or not he will heal my body. Not at all. My belief hangs on his character and promises.

Happy and I pray for healing and for my days to be extended almost every night. Amidst these prayers, we also ask for trust, regardless of the outcome. Our prayers for trust and the peace that is its outcome seems more important than the prayers for healing. Our confidence in God doesn't rely solely on what he does for us. It is rooted much deeper. The challenge of this season is to live gloriously day-by-day and not waste the good days.

My calling remains to be a good husband, father, grandfather, friend, coach, and mentor—to love my neighbors as God called me to.

There is nothing I have learned through cancer and chemo that isn't available to everyone who follows Jesus. While my circumstances have sharpened my focus, the lessons are universal—true in all times, places, cultures, and systems. Being near the finish line enriches our living. Since everyone has a finish line, everyone has this opportunity.

Happy and I pray that each of you will, in your own time, come to Christ. These emails are meant to invite you behind the curtain, to understand how we think and trust, to see where our strength is anchored, and where we find peace and confidence. There is much about these days that is hard for both Happy and me. But there is also much that is rich, beautiful, and good. Each of you is part of the best part of these days. I hope you will see that you can trust the same God your grandparents have trusted. We find stability and confidence in him alone.

I hope I've shown enough of my true self to help you. I want you to understand what we leaned on when life became very hard. I want you to know what we believe and trust. Life will undoubtedly present you with moments when everything seems overwhelming, and you feel you are at the end of your strength. In those moments, remember this: God is with you. Trusting him takes courage, but he is the creator of courage. Lean on him as we have, and you will find the strength to endure and the peace that only he gives.

> **Live with purpose.**
>
> **Love deeply.**
>
> **Seek truth and**
>
> **cherish beauty.**

Live with purpose. Love deeply. Seek truth and cherish beauty. Let your life be a testament to the grace and love of God. Be a beacon of hope and compassion in a world that so desperately needs it. Know that you are part of a legacy of faith, one that is anchored in the unwavering goodness of God. Embrace the journey. Yes, sorrow is bound up with love. Yes, we will face situations we did not ask for, but in all of life, there is grandeur and glory, even in the hard parts. Happy and I believe that in all circumstances we can find a way to live gloriously.

With all my love and blessings,
Pops

ACKNOWLEDGMENTS

No one "writes a book" by themselves. There are always many people without whom a book would not exist. *Courage Required* is no exception.

Many people have encouraged me to write this book for a long time, even without knowing what it would look like. Their encouragement stemmed from a personal belief that I would have something valuable to say once I began. One Christmas, my sister gave me a framed picture that said, "Write the book you want to read." It was one of her last of many encouragements through the years. My dear friend Regi Campbell consistently inspired me in my work and in writing this book. Kurt Kandler, as is his habit, provided the vision for the book by suggesting that it should mirror our conversations at "Eggs Up Grill." Many other friends and clients supported me in this endeavor. Most were consistent and gentle, while a few were more insistent and pushy. I treasure all of them.

To be clear, *Courage Required* would never have been either started or finished without my wife, Martha. From long ago until today, she has been a consistent advocate and encourager. Her indispensable voice prompted and sustained the process. I am so thankful for her.

The folks at Streamline Books, especially Cindy McCachern, were indispensable in bringing this book to life. I will always owe a debt to Cindy for her creative insights and editing of my jumbled ideas that moved this book from the invisible world of my mind into the visible book you are reading. Cindy's innovative effort in developing the book's form was pivotal and essential. Streamline, as a whole, made the process of producing a book incredibly easy. They have been a joy to work with.

I have been mentoring and coaching men for seventeen years, with most of these relationships being long-term. These men have honored me by welcoming me into their businesses and lives month after month, year after year. We have few secrets left between us. I have witnessed both great success and profound pain. It is a privilege and joy that I have never taken lightly and continue to hold in high regard. This group of men is central to *Courage Required*. Many of the ideas in this book stem from extensive conversations with the men I coach. This book would not have been possible without them.

Like everyone else, I stand on the shoulders of those who have come before me. There are too many to list here, but I have been blessed to be taught and mentored by many talented and thoughtful individuals. I doubt I have ever had an entirely original thought. As the apostle Paul asked the Corinthian church, "What do you have that you did not receive?" In my case, the answer is...nothing.

ABOUT THE AUTHOR

John and his wife Martha have lived in Marietta, Georgia, a suburb of Atlanta, since 1984. They raised their three children here, all of whom are now happily married. John and Martha are known as Happy and Pops to their nine talented and remarkable grandchildren.

Both John and Martha have been dedicated mentors through their church, Johnson Ferry, for many years. John has completed mentoring four groups, while Martha has led fourteen. This experience inspired their purpose statement: "To invest in the next generation to the glory of God."

After a career as an executive, John transitioned to becoming an executive coach in 2006. This has been his longest and most rewarding tenure. Most of the men that John works with are CEOs of their businesses. He writes for the group every month and publishes a weekly "Wisdom Book," sharing the smart or wise ideas he has encountered.

In 2022 John was diagnosed with cancer and underwent surgery followed by six months of chemotherapy. The cancer returned in 2023, and he is currently participating in a clinical trial at Vanderbilt Medical Center in Nashville. Despite these challenges, he maintains a full coaching schedule and is preparing to launch his next mentoring group with his co-mentor.

ENDNOTES

1 Richard Rohr, *Falling Upward: A Spirituality for the Two Halves of Life* (San Francisco: Jossey-Bass, 2011).

2 Timothy Keller, *Every Good Endeavor: Connecting Your Work to God's Work* (New York: Dutton, 2012), 12.

3 Joe Ehrmann, "Radical Mentoring Speech," 2012.

4 Martin Luther, *Luther's Works*, Volume 44: The Christian in Society IV, ed. Jaroslav Jan Pelikan, Hilton C. Oswald, and Helmut T. Lehmann (Philadelphia: Fortress Press, 1966), 123.

5 World Bank, "A Global Count of the Extreme Poor in 2012," October 2015, accessed June 15, 2024, https://www.worldbank.org/en/topic/poverty/overview.

6 Søren Kierkegaard, *The Sickness Unto Death*, as explained by Gordon Marino in "Your Three Selves and How Not to Fall Into Despair," The Art of Manliness, accessed June 15, 2024, https://www.artofmanliness.com/articles/your-three-selves-and-how-not-to-fall-into-despair/.

7 Daniel Nayeri, *Everything Sad Is Untrue: (A True Story)* (New York: Levine Querido, 2020).

8 Viktor E. Frankl, *Man's Search for Meaning* (Boston: Beacon Press, 2006), 85.

9 John Piper, *Don't Waste Your Life* (Wheaton, IL: Crossway Books, 2003), 45-48.

10 Clayton Christensen, *How Do You Measure Your Life?* (New York: HarperBusiness, 2012).

11 Clayton Christensen, *The Innovator's Dilemma: When New Technologies Cause Great Firms to Fail* (Boston: Harvard Business Review Press, 1997).

12 Henry Cloud, *9 Things You Simply Must Do to Succeed in Love and Life* (Nashville: Thomas Nelson, 2004).

13 The concept of the cycle of change, which includes phases like execution, doldrums, cocooning, and planning, is well-documented in the field of personal and professional development. This model is closely related to the Cycle of Renewal identified by the Hudson Institute of Santa Barbara.

14 Sigmund Freud, *Beyond the Pleasure Principle*, 1920, accessed June 15, 2024, https://www.sigmundfreud.net/beyond-the-pleasure-principle/.

15 Friedrich Nietzsche, *Thus Spoke Zarathustra*, trans. Walter Kaufmann (New York: Penguin Books, 1978).

16 Viktor Frankl, *Man's Search for Meaning* (Boston: Beacon Press, 2006).

17 Jim Rohn, *The Treasury of Quotes*, (Southlake, TX: Jim Rohn International, 1997), 35.

18 Charles Dickens, *A Christmas Carol* (London: Chapman & Hall, 1843).

19 *Gladiator*, directed by Ridley Scott (2000; Universal Pictures and DreamWorks Pictures), Netflix.

20 Robin Dunbar, *How Many Friends Does One Person Need?: Dunbar's Number and Other Evolutionary Quirks* (Cambridge, MA: Harvard University Press, 2010).

21 Robertson McQuilkin, *A Promise Kept* (Carol Stream, IL: Tyndale House Publishers, 1998).

22 Thomas Cole, *The Voyage of Life: Manhood*, 1842, oil on canvas, National Gallery of Art, Washington, D.C.

23 George Swinnock, *The Christian Man's Calling*, ed. William Symonds (London: John Grismond for Nathanael Webb and William Grantham, 1662), 104.

24 John Eldredge, *Resilient: Restoring Your Weary Soul in These Turbulent Times* (Nashville: Thomas Nelson, 2022).

25 Martin Luther, *Luther's Works*, Volume 44: The Christian in Society IV, ed. Jaroslav Jan Pelikan, Hilton C. Oswald, and Helmut T. Lehmann (Philadelphia: Fortress Press, 1966), 123.

26 Erik H. Erikson, *Identity: Youth and Crisis* (New York: W. W. Norton & Company, 1968).

27 John Emerich Edward Dalberg-Acton, *Historical Essays and Studies*, edited by J.N. Figgis and R.V. Laurence (London: Macmillan, 1907). This book includes the letter where Acton famously wrote this phrase.

28 Douglas Southall Freeman, *Lee's Lieutenants* (New York: Charles Scribner's Sons, 1942), viii.

29 Marcus Aurelius, *Meditations*, translated by Gregory Hays (New York: Modern Library, 2002).

30 John Lewis, *Walking with the Wind: A Memoir of the Movement* (New York: Simon & Schuster, 1998).

31 Henri Nouwen, *The Inner Voice of Love: A Journey Through Anguish to Freedom* (New York: Doubleday, 1996).

32 Robert Waldinger, *"What Makes a Good Life? Lessons from the Longest Study on Happiness,"* TED Talk, 2015, and *"The Contagion of Happiness,"* Harvard Medicine Magazine, Winter 2017, https://magazine.hms.harvard.edu/articles/contagion-happiness.

33 Henry Cloud, *"Ultimate Leadership Seminar,"* Laguna Beach, CA, 2014.

34 Robin Dunbar, *How Many Friends Does One Person Need? Dunbar's Number and Other Evolutionary Quirks* (Cambridge, MA: Harvard University Press, 2010).

35 Winston Churchill, eulogy for Neville Chamberlain, House of Commons, November 12, 1940, in *The Unrelenting Struggle: War Speeches by the Right Hon. Winston S. Churchill C.H., M.P.*, comp. Charles Eade (Boston: Little, Brown and Company, 1942), 256-257.

36 "Chinese Proverb," Your Positive Oasis, accessed June 13, 2024, https://yourpositiveoasis.com/35-wonderful-chinese-proverbs/.

37 Dietrich Bonhoeffer, *Life Together*, trans. John W. Doberstein (New York: Harper & Row, 1954), 23.

38 Phillip Brooks, *The Life and Letters of Phillips Brooks*, ed. Alexander V.G. Allen (New York: E.P. Dutton & Co., 1900), 337.

39 J.R.R. Tolkien, *The Fellowship of the Ring* (Boston: Houghton Mifflin, 1954), 365.

40 Abby Wambach, *WOLFPACK: How to Come Together, Unleash Our Power, and Change the Game* (New York: Celadon Books, 2019).

41 Alex Scarborough, "Georgia Bulldogs Defeat Alabama Crimson Tide for First College Football National Title Since 1980," ESPN, January 11, 2022, accessed June 17, 2024, https://www.espn.com/college-football/recap/_/gameId/401403911.

42 Bill Gates, as quoted in "Setting the Stage: Technology and the Modern Enterprise," Saylor Academy, accessed June 15, 2024, https://saylordotorg.github.io/text_leading-strategically/s03-types-of-ceos.html.

43 David Wilcox, "All the Roots Grow Deeper When It's Dry," *Big Horizon*, UMG Recordings, 1994. Available on Apple Music, accessed June 15, 2024, https://music.apple.com/us/album/all-the-roots-grow-deeper-when-its-dry/1994.

44 Gordon MacDonald, interview by Steve Macchia, "Gordon MacDonald Part 1 | Your Discerning Life Story, Episode 5," The

Discerning Leader Podcast, April 28, 2022, Leadership Transformations. https://www.leadershiptransformations.org/podcast/episode5.

45 Frederick Buechner, Now and Then: A Memoir of Vocation (New York: HarperOne, 1991), 87.

46 Mark Vroegop, Dark Clouds, Deep Mercy: Discovering the Grace of Lament (Wheaton, IL: Crossway, 2019).

47 St. Augustine, Ten Homilies on the First Epistle of John, in Nicene and Post-Nicene Fathers, First Series, vol. 7, ed. Philip Schaff (Buffalo, NY: Christian Literature Publishing Co., 1888), rev. Kevin Knight, accessed June 14, 2024, https://www.newadvent.org/fathers/170207.htm.

48 Dietrich Bonhoeffer, Life Together: The Classic Exploration of Christian Community, trans. John W. Doberstein (New York: Harper & Row, 1954), 112.

www.ingramcontent.com/pod-product-compliance
Lightning Source LLC
Chambersburg PA
CBHW021152130626
46554CB00005B/1784